BUNNY OF APPROVAL™

Annie's™

The Cookbook

Bacon Avocado Mac & Cheese (page 130)

The Cookbook

Recipes Everybunny Will Love

ANNIE'S

HARVEST

An Imprint of WILLIAM MORROW

GENERAL MILLS

Director, Brand Experience Creative: Melissa
    Wildermuth

Manager, Brand Experience Creative—Food
    Licensing, Partnerships & Ideas: Lisa Balzo

Executive Editor/Food Editor: Cathy
    Swanson Wheaton

Recipe Development and Testing: Betty
    Crocker Kitchens

Photography: General Mills Photography
    Studios and Tony Kubat Photography

Photographer: ReGina Murphy

Photo Assistants: Maren Woolhouse,
    Maya Bolduan

Food Stylists: Carol Grones, Amy Peterson

Food Styling Assistant: Jerry Dudycha

Prop Stylist: Michele Joy

HARVEST

Vice President and Editorial Director:
    Deb Brody

Senior Editor: Sarah Kwak

Managing Editor: Jennifer Eck

Production Editorial Manager: Rachel Meyers

Senior Production Editor: Shelby Peak

Cover Design: Olivia LoSardo

Interior Design: Melissa Lotfy and Tai Blanche

Senior Production Associate: Chris Andrus

Dietary icons: © Sudowoodo/Shutterstock

HarperCollins books may be purchased for
educational, business, or sales promotional
use. For information, please email the
Special Markets Department at SPsales@
harpercollins.com.

FIRST EDITION

Library of Congress Cataloging-in-Publication
Data has been applied for.

ISBN 978-0-06-330858-9

23 24 25 26 27 TC 10 9 8 7 6 5 4 3 2 1

Inspiring America to Cook at Home™

Learn more about
Annie's nourishing foods
at annies.com.

Letter from the Editors

Welcome to Goodness!

We've been busy bunnies here at Annie's, cultivating a healthier, happier world by nourishing families with down-to-earth foods that taste delicious and are made from simple, real ingredients. Now you can enjoy carefree, wholesome foods all day with the recipes inside. From **Yummy Breakfasts** or **Shareable Snacks,** to **Delicious Dinners Together** or **Sweets to Bring Smiles,** these are tasty dishes everybunny will love and ask for.

Nobunny should be left out—so if you or someone you love has dietary restrictions, look for recipes **made without dairy** 🥛 **or nut** 🥜 **ingredients, gluten free** GF **, vegetarian** V **, or vegan** V+ . These are so tasty; everyone can enjoy them. Peek at the feature in each chapter that adds delightful fun to your cooking and eating, including **Hack Your Mac** and **Fun between Dinner and Dessert**.

Then snuggle in and read the **Farm to Fork Stories** sprinkled throughout, which tell the story of how organic, sustainable farming brings foods to your table that are not only good for you but also good for the planet.

Hoppy eating (and reading),
ALL OF US AT ANNIE'S

Contents

♥

The Annie's Story viii

Yummy Breakfasts 5
Making Breakfast Together 30

Shareable Snacks 53

Joyful Surprise Bento Boxes 70

Delicious Dinners Together 95
Hack Your Mac 124

Sweets to Bring Smiles 143
Fun between Dinner and Dessert 172

Bibliography 194

Index 195

The

Annie's™

STORY

Hop-along for a look back at the history of Annie's, where our mission has always been at the forefront of what we do: to cultivate a **HEALTHIER** and **HAPPIER** world by spreading goodness through nourishing foods, honest words, and conduct that is considerate and forever kind to the planet.

In 1989, Annie Withey believed it was possible to build a socially conscious and successful business when she cofounded the company, making mac & cheese and selling it from the trunk of her car. The very first boxes of Annie's macaroni & cheese had her name, address, and phone number on them.

In the early days, we also launched a product donation program, Cases for Causes, delivering cases of the delicious mac & cheese to local community centers, schools, and various organizations that benefit women, children, education, and the environment.

Annie Withey's legacy lives on as we strive to change the future for our kids, starting with food. At our core, Annie's is a company built on an ever-deepening commitment to bettering the world. It began with natural ingredients and continued with the first mac & cheese product to be all organic.

Sowing the seeds of goodness, for more than a decade we offered a Sustainable Agricultural Scholarship program. It assisted undergraduate and graduate students pursuing studies in sustainable and organic agriculture.

In 2008, a partnership was formed with Organic Valley, an independent cooperative of organic farmers, to source organic dairy for Annie's products.

In 2014, Annie's joined the General Mills team, where we are committed to grow better together and scale our mission to build a better future for families and the planet.

The culture at Annie's has always been to listen to our customers. Over time, Annie's has branched out into more than 15 food categories, including fruit snacks, crackers, baking mixes, and more, to give even more families upgraded options across the supermarket.

Bernie, the official Annie's mascot, has always graced Annie's packaging, giving his blessing to all products with the "Bunny of Approval" stamp. He shows up in bunny-shaped products and hopping hoppily through Annie's photography and messaging. How many places can you find Bernie and his other bunny friends in this book?

For more information, visit us at annies.com.

Yummy Breakfasts

Agriculture for What We Eat

Agriculture is the most important industry in the world—as it makes the food that people and animals eat! It's the science and practice of growing crops and the raising of animals to provide food and other products.

Farming is also called agriculture. Farming is directly connected to nature and to you. Farmers who grow the food you eat use the biodiversity and natural resources found in nature (like seeds, soil, and water), as well as machinery like tractors, to plant, grow, and harvest food for people or animals to eat.

Fruity Alphabet Pancakes

PREP TIME: 30 Minutes ● **START TO FINISH:** 30 Minutes ● 4 servings
(2 pancakes, ¼ cup sauce, ½ cup fruit each)

Strawberry Sauce
1 package (10 oz) frozen sliced
strawberries, thawed
1 tablespoon honey

Pancakes
1 cup oat milk
1 tablespoon canola oil
1 tablespoon honey
1 egg
1 cup white whole wheat flour
2 teaspoons chia seeds
1½ teaspoons baking powder
¼ teaspoon salt

Toppings
1 ripe large peach, peeled and
sliced, or 1 cup frozen sliced
peaches, thawed
1 cup sliced fresh strawberries

1 In blender or food processor, place strawberries. Cover; process
strawberries about 30 seconds or until smooth. Pour into 2-cup
microwavable measuring cup; stir in 1 tablespoon honey. Cover;
microwave on High 30 seconds; stir. Microwave 30 seconds or
until hot.

2 Heat nonstick griddle or skillet over medium heat or electric griddle
to 350°F; brush lightly with oil, if necessary.

3 In medium bowl, beat milk, oil, 1 tablespoon honey, and egg with
whisk until well blended. Beat in flour, chia seeds, baking powder, and
salt just until smooth. Place about ¼ cup batter into 1-pint resealable
food-storage plastic bag. Cut ½ inch from the end of one corner of
the bag. Set aside remaining batter.

4 For each pancake, pipe batter onto hot griddle to form a 2½-inch-tall
letter, leaving 4 inches between letters to make pancakes. (Letters

recipe continues

must be made backward to make them appear "right" when pancakes are served.) Cook 30 seconds or until bottoms are golden brown. Quickly pour a scant ¼ cup of additional batter over letter, spreading batter to make 4-inch pancake. Cook 1 to 2 minutes or until dry around edges and bubbles begin to form on top; turn with nonstick pancake turner. Cook other side 1 to 2 minutes or until golden brown. (If the pancake batter in the bowl gets too thick to spread nicely, stir in an additional tablespoon of oat milk.)

5 Serve pancakes with sauce and sliced peaches and strawberries.

1 Serving Calories 300; Total Fat 7g (Saturated Fat 1g, Trans Fat 0g); Cholesterol 45mg; Sodium 380mg; Total Carbohydrate 51g (Dietary Fiber 7g); Protein 8g **Carbohydrate Choices:** 3½

Cooking without Dairy or Nut Ingredients? Always read labels to make sure each ingredient is made without dairy or nuts. Products, ingredients, and processing methods can change.

Where Does Food Come From?

Nearly all the food we eat started out as plants grown on farms. When plants are grown to feed people or animals, they are called crops. Some crops, like fruits and vegetables, can be eaten right after they are harvested, but others need to be processed first. For example, the macaroni in your mac & cheese comes from crops like wheat, which is turned into flour, which is then transformed into macaroni.

scrumptiously
whole-grain

Almond butter–infused pancakes have great texture and flavor, with a nutty crunch ya can't resist. Some almond butters are textured; others are smooth and creamy. Pick your favorite to use in this recipe.

Nutty Almond Butter Pancakes

PREP TIME: 25 Minutes • **START TO FINISH:** 25 Minutes • 8 servings (2 pancakes each with toppings)

Pancakes
2 cups Annie's organic Classic pancake & waffle mix (from 26-oz box)
1 cup milk
½ cup creamy almond butter
¼ cup sugar
2 eggs

Toppings
4 ripe medium bananas, sliced
2 cups fresh blueberries
⅓ cup chopped almonds
Additional creamy almond butter, if desired
Pure maple syrup, if desired

1 Heat nonstick griddle or skillet over medium heat (350°F); brush lightly with canola oil, if necessary.

2 In medium bowl, beat all pancake ingredients with whisk until well mixed. If batter seems too thick, add an additional 1 to 2 tablespoons milk.

3 For each pancake, pour ¼ cup batter onto hot griddle. Cook 1 to 2 minutes or until dry around edges and bubbles begin to form on top; turn with nonstick pancake turner. Cook other side 1 to 2 minutes or until golden brown. Place 2 pancakes on each serving plate; top with ½ sliced banana, ¼ cup blueberries, and scant tablespoon almonds. Serve with almond butter and maple syrup.

1 Serving Calories 380; Total Fat 15g (Saturated Fat 1.5g, Trans Fat 0g); Cholesterol 50mg; Sodium 310mg; Total Carbohydrate 52g (Dietary Fiber 5g); Protein 10g **Carbohydrate Choices:** 3½

photo on next page

Grow a Garden

You don't need a huge farm field to grow food. Gardens can come in lots of shapes and sizes. Start by looking around your home for something to "house" your plants. You don't need anything fancy—a flowerpot or even an empty milk jug or plastic food container can be used to grow plants. Then take a walk around your home or yard to find a nice, sunny spot for your plants to grow. Carve out a spot on your balcony or porch for a tomato plant; build a raised garden bed and plant lettuce, cucumbers, or watermelons; or even find a sunny windowsill to grow an herb garden. Make sure your plants have enough to drink (water) and eat (healthy soil) and then help harvest and prepare a meal with them. You'll be deliciously proud of your efforts.

Nutty Almond Butter
Pancakes

This yummy combination of flavors is perfect for a family breakfast, brunch, or even breakfast for dinner.

Oatmeal Pancakes

PREP TIME: 15 Minutes • **START TO FINISH:** 15 Minutes • 6 servings (3 pancakes, ¼ cup blueberries, 2 teaspoons coconut, 2 tablespoons syrup each)

Pancakes
2 cups Annie's organic Classic pancake & waffle mix (from 26-oz box)
1¼ cups milk
½ cup old-fashioned or quick-cooking oats
2 tablespoons sugar
2 eggs

Toppings
1½ cups fresh blueberries
¼ cup unsweetened large coconut flakes, toasted
¾ cup pure maple syrup

1 Heat nonstick griddle or skillet over medium heat (350°F); brush lightly with canola oil, if necessary.

2 In medium bowl, beat all pancake ingredients with whisk until well mixed. If batter seems too thick, add an additional 1 to 2 tablespoons milk.

3 For each pancake, pour slightly less than ¼ cup batter onto hot griddle. Cook 1 to 2 minutes or until dry around edges and bubbles begin to form on top; turn with nonstick pancake turner. Cook other side 1 to 2 minutes or until golden brown. Top pancakes with blueberries and coconut flakes. Serve with maple syrup.

1 Serving Calories 360; Total Fat 6g (Saturated Fat 2.5g, Trans Fat 0g); Cholesterol 65mg; Sodium 380mg; Total Carbohydrate 69g (Dietary Fiber 2g); Protein 8g **Carbohydrate Choices:** 4½

The deep pockets of Belgian waffles make lovely little spots for toppings to hang out, so ya can have yumminess in every bite.

Belgian Waffles

PREP TIME: 5 Minutes ● **START TO FINISH:** 25 Minutes ● 4 servings

Waffles

2 cups Annie's organic Classic pancake & waffle mix (from 26-oz box)

1⅓ cups milk

2 tablespoons canola oil

1 egg

Toppings

2 cups fresh mixed berries

1 container (5.3 oz) nonfat Greek vanilla yogurt

Powdered sugar, if desired

1 Heat Belgian waffle iron; brush with canola oil or spray with cooking spray, if necessary.

2 In medium bowl, beat all waffle ingredients with whisk until blended.

3 For each waffle, pour scant 1 cup batter onto center of hot waffle maker. (Check manufacturer's directions for recommended amount of batter.) Close lid of waffle maker.

4 Bake about 4 minutes or until steaming stops. Carefully remove waffle. Top each waffle with ½ cup berries and 2 tablespoons yogurt. Sprinkle with powdered sugar. Serve immediately.

> **Easy Cooking Tip** Sprinkle the waffles lightly with powdered sugar by placing a teaspoon or two in a small fine-mesh strainer. Tap the edge of the strainer with a spoon over the waffles.

1 Serving Calories 370; Total Fat 12g (Saturated Fat 2g, Trans Fat 0g); Cholesterol 55mg; Sodium 560mg; Total Carbohydrate 52g (Dietary Fiber 4g); Protein 13g **Carbohydrate Choices:** 3½

Try mixing and matching fruit for a fun wake-me-up breakfast. Use what ya have on hand. Try any combo of berries, kiwifruit, bananas, melon, pineapple, or oranges.

Cinnamon Roll Waffles

PREP TIME: 15 Minutes • **START TO FINISH:** 15 Minutes • 5 servings

1 can (17.5 oz) refrigerated Annie's organic cinnamon rolls with icing (5 count)

2 tablespoons whole milk or nonfat Greek vanilla yogurt

1¼ cups assorted fresh berries or cut-up fruit

3 tablespoons strawberry or raspberry fruit spread

1 Spray waffle maker with cooking spray; heat waffle maker. Separate dough into 5 rolls; set icing aside.

2 For each waffle, flatten roll slightly with hand to 3½-inch diameter. Place roll in center of waffle maker; close lid of waffle maker. Bake 1 to 1½ minutes or until waffle is thoroughly cooked and golden brown (watch carefully so waffles don't burn). Place waffle on heatproof serving dish; loosely cover to keep warm. Repeat with remaining rolls.

3 In small bowl, stir icing packet and yogurt until blended. Drizzle over waffles. Spoon ¼ cup fruit over each waffle. In small microwavable bowl, place fruit spread. Microwave uncovered on High 15 to 30 seconds or just until mixture can be stirred to drizzling consistency. Drizzle over fruit. Serve immediately.

1 Serving Calories 380; Total Fat 11g (Saturated Fat 4.5g, Trans Fat 0g); Cholesterol 0mg; Sodium 750mg; Total Carbohydrate 64g (Dietary Fiber 3g); Protein 4g **Carbohydrate Choices:** 4

On busy days, when your bunnies are hopping out the door, send them off with this tummy-filling twist on toast. The peanut butter is thick enough to stay on the waffles and hold the crumbled granola bars, but you could substitute a nut butter instead. It will just have a thinner consistency.

PB (and) J Waffle Toast

PREP TIME: 15 Minutes ● **START TO FINISH:** 15 Minutes ● 4 servings

4 Annie's organic frozen Homestyle or Blueberry waffles (from 9.8-oz box)
½ cup creamy peanut butter
¼ cup blueberry fruit spread

4 teaspoons water
2 Annie's organic Chocolate Chip chewy granola bars, crumbled (from 5.34-oz box)

1 Heat waffles as directed on package. Spread 2 tablespoons peanut butter on each waffle.

2 In small microwavable bowl, mix fruit spread and water. Microwave uncovered on High 30 seconds or just until mixture can be stirred until smooth. Spoon over top of waffles. Sprinkle with granola bars. Serve immediately.

1 Serving Calories 360; Total Fat 20g (Saturated Fat 4g, Trans Fat 0g); Cholesterol 0mg; Sodium 340mg; Total Carbohydrate 37g (Dietary Fiber 2g); Protein 9g **Carbohydrate Choices:** 2½

What Are Crops?

Crops are plants that grow from the earth, like fruits, vegetables, and grains. Farmers grow and harvest crops, which are then sold at the market or become ingredients that food companies use to make products for people and animals to eat.

**tasty
tummy filler**

The sweet and savory flavors of Monte Cristo sandwiches are made super easy with waffles.

Monte Cristo Wafflewiches

PREP TIME: 15 Minutes ● **START TO FINISH:** 15 Minutes ● 4 servings (2 wedges each)

4 Annie's organic frozen Homestyle waffles (from 9.8-oz box)

2 tablespoons mayonnaise

2 teaspoons Dijon mustard

4 slices (¾ oz each) Swiss cheese

6 very thin slices cooked deli ham (about 3 oz)

6 very thin slices cooked deli turkey breast (about 3 oz)

2 tablespoons strawberry fruit spread

1 teaspoon powdered sugar

Additional strawberry fruit spread, if desired

1 Heat waffles in oven as directed on package.

2 Meanwhile, in small bowl, stir together mayonnaise and mustard until smooth.

3 Spread mayonnaise mixture on one side of 2 waffles. Top each with 1 slice cheese, 3 slices ham, 3 slices turkey, and 1 slice cheese. Spread the fruit spread on one side of remaining 2 waffles; place fruit spread side down on sandwiches.

4 Cut each waffle sandwich into 4 wedges. If desired, secure wedges with a toothpick and place on baking pan. Heat in oven 3 to 5 minutes or just until cheese begins to melt. Place wedges on serving plates; remove toothpicks and sprinkle with powdered sugar. Serve with additional fruit spread.

1 Serving Calories 320; Total Fat 17g (Saturated Fat 5g, Trans Fat 0g); Cholesterol 45mg; Sodium 860mg; Total Carbohydrate 27g (Dietary Fiber 1g); Protein 15g **Carbohydrate Choices:** 2

All about Corn

When you think about corn, you probably think about eating popcorn or corn on the cob. Did you know that corn is the most widely grown crop in the United States? That's because corn is often used as an ingredient in lots of other foods and drinks. We also need a lot of corn to feed the animals we raise for meat, milk, and eggs. When meat, milk, or eggs are labeled organic, it means that the corn eaten by the animals (if any) was grown on an organic farm. Organic corn is grown without chemical fertilizers and chemical pesticides.

Choose your favorite artisan nut-free multigrain bread with a dense texture for this recipe so the sticks can stand up to the batter without falling apart. Little fingers will love taking their sticks for a dip in the fruity sauce.

Churro French Toast Sticks
with Berry Sauce

PREP TIME: 30 Minutes • **START TO FINISH:** 30 Minutes • 4 servings (6 sticks, ¼ cup sauce, and 1 teaspoon topping each)

Churro Topping
4 teaspoons sugar
¼ teaspoon ground cinnamon

Berry Sauce
2 cups frozen berry blend or frozen strawberries, thawed (from 15-oz bag)
1 tablespoon honey

French Toast Sticks
¾ cup unsweetened vanilla coconut milk
3 eggs
1 teaspoon vanilla
8 slices firm-textured nut-free multigrain bread, cut into thirds

1 In small bowl, stir together sugar and cinnamon until blended; set aside.

2 In food processor, place berries. Cover; process berries about 30 seconds or until smooth. Pour into 2-cup microwavable measuring cup; stir in honey. Cover; microwave on High 2 minutes 30 seconds, stirring after 1 minute, or until hot. Set aside.

3 Heat griddle or skillet over medium heat or electric griddle to 350°F. Spray griddle with cooking spray, if necessary.

4 In shallow bowl or pie plate, beat all French toast stick ingredients except bread with fork until smooth. Dip bread sticks in egg mixture, coating both sides; drain excess batter back into bowl.

recipe continues

yummy
goodness

5 Place bread sticks on griddle. Cook about 1 minute on each side or until golden brown. Remove from griddle; place on serving plate. Sprinkle with churro topping; serve with warm sauce.

1 Serving Calories 340; Total Fat 8g (Saturated Fat 2.5g, Trans Fat 0g); Cholesterol 140mg; Sodium 330mg; Total Carbohydrate 51g (Dietary Fiber 8g); Protein 15g **Carbohydrate Choices:** 3½

Cooking without Dairy or Nut Ingredients? Always read labels to make sure each ingredient is made without nuts. Products, ingredients, and processing methods can change.

What Can a Farmer Grow?

What farms produce depends on many things, such as what the growing conditions are like in the farm's area. This includes climate, length of daylight, soil type, rainfall and water, and more. Different types of crops grow well in different regions of the country and the world. Oranges grow well in places that are sunny and warm year-round while other crops, like oats, will grow well only in cooler places.

No ordinary French toast, this deluxe version is filled with apple, chicken sausage, and cream cheese for an over-the-top morning experience.

Apple-and-Sausage-Stuffed French Toast

PREP TIME: 30 Minutes • **START TO FINISH:** 30 Minutes • 4 servings

8 slices gluten-free, nut-free cinnamon, 7-grain, or white bread

⅓ cup plain cream cheese spread (from 8-oz container)

¼ teaspoon ground cinnamon

1 medium red or green apple, thinly sliced

4 fully cooked chicken-apple sausage links (from 12-oz package), heated as directed, cut in half lengthwise

1 egg

¼ cup milk

1 teaspoon vanilla

¼ teaspoon salt

Pure maple syrup, if desired

1 Spread one side of each bread slice with cream cheese; sprinkle with cinnamon. In small microwavable bowl, place apples. Microwave uncovered on High 30 seconds or until just slightly softened. On 4 slices of the bread, cream cheese side up, arrange apple slices and sausage. Top with remaining bread slices, cream cheese side down.

2 Spray griddle with cooking spray; heat griddle to 300°F.

3 In shallow bowl or pie plate, beat egg, milk, vanilla, and salt with whisk until smooth. Working with 1 stuffed French toast at a time, dip bottom of French toast into egg mixture to cover bread slice; let stand 10 seconds. Repeat on other side. Place on griddle. Repeat with remaining stuffed French toast and milk mixture. Cook 2 to 3 minutes on each side or until golden brown. Cut into quarters. Serve with maple syrup.

1 Serving Calories 330; Total Fat 16g (Saturated Fat 6g, Trans Fat 0g); Cholesterol 85mg; Sodium 660mg; Total Carbohydrate 36g (Dietary Fiber 3g); Protein 10g **Carbohydrate Choices:** 2½

Made without Nut Ingredients? Always read labels to make sure each ingredient is made without nuts. Products, ingredients, and processing methods can change.

Cooking Gluten Free? Always read labels to make sure each recipe ingredient is gluten free. Products and ingredient sources can change.

Making Breakfast Together

What could be more special than bonding with your kiddo while making breakfast together? It's the yummiest teachable moment ever. Little bunnies learn basic kitchen skills and safety while also learning math and science. As kids build on their skills, they become more independent and confident. And to top it all off . . . you get to eat the homework.

Pick a Lazy, Not a Crazy Day

Weekend brunch is a perfect time to spend cooking. There's time to wake up and caffeinate before the mixing bowls make it out of the cupboard. If you're relaxed, your kids will be too . . . setting yourself up for some memorable fun times.

Start with Hands and Eyes

Teach good hygiene . . . always wash your hands first: Share joy, not germs, right? Read through the recipe together. You can read it to them when they're small or have them read it to you when they're old enough to do so.

Play with Your Food

Let the pint-size chefs get out all the ingredients for the recipe. It will help them learn where everything is (and cuts down on the "Mom, where's the ___?" questions over time). Turn on the tunes; dance and explore! Let them open packages, touch, smell, and taste the ingredients, when possible. Their natural curiosity will get them excited about what you're about to create.

Embrace the Mess

Spills will happen . . . only with practice can bunnies improve. Minimize any chaos with a few tricks: When measuring milk, if they're too small to handle a gallon jug, give them a small pitcher to pour milk from. Work over a 15×10×1-inch pan when using things like cinnamon or sprinkles, keeping them contained. Cooking means cleanup—have your little bunnies hop to helping here also. It's bonus time and skills learned.

Build Their Skills

We love the Fruity Alphabet Pancake recipe (page 7), as it offers skills even the tiniest chefs can practice! Bitty bunnies can learn their letters while learning to cook at the same time. Always supervise younger children using kitchen appliances, ovens, or stove tops.

Skills for Everybunny by Age

BABY BUNNIES
(2–5 YEARS)

Clear counters

Cut out cookies with cookie cutters

Fill measuring cups

Mix pancake batter

Rinse and strain fresh fruit and vegetables

Vacuum crumbs with handheld vacuum

BUDDING BUNNIES
(6–8 YEARS)

Beat eggs

Boil eggs and pasta

Flip pancakes

Frost cupcakes and cookies

Load dishwasher

Melt chocolate in microwave

Peel fruits and vegetables with vegetable peeler

Sweep floors

Wash counter

TWEEN BUNNIES
(9–12 YEARS)

Bake muffins or cupcakes

Draw pancake letters with batter; cook pancakes

Knead dough

Load/Unload dishwasher

Operate small appliances like food processor, blender, stand mixer, waffle maker

Cut with large knife

Wash, dry, and put away dishes

Mop floor

Put back ingredients in pantry

TEEN BUNNIES
(13–16 YEARS)

Bake yeast doughs

Chop, dice with large knife

Clean blender and food processor with sharp blades

Cook over stove (panfry, stir-fry, etc.)

Marinate meats and vegetables

Organize pantry

Prepare main dish or dessert

Set the table

Trim fruits and vegetables with small knife

Use and clean oven and grill

Fruity Alphabet Pancakes (page 7)

These cute bunnies are sure to make breakfast a hoppy surprise and delight.

Fruity Bunny Cinnamon Rolls

PREP TIME: 20 Minutes ● **START TO FINISH:** 40 Minutes ● 5 rolls

1 can (17.5 oz) refrigerated Annie's organic cinnamon rolls with icing (5 count)

¼ cup raspberry fruit spread

2 oz cream cheese, softened (from 8-oz package)

1 tablespoon milk

10 raisins, sweetened cranberries, or candy-coated chocolate pieces

1 package Annie's organic fruit Strawberry Splits Peel-A-Parts, separated into strips, cut in half (from 3.3-oz box)

1 Heat oven to 350°F. Grease or spray cookie sheet with cooking spray.

2 Separate cinnamon roll dough into 5 rolls; set icing aside. Unroll each roll, almost completely, into a long dough strip. Reserve ¼ teaspoon of fruit spread; set aside. Spoon scant 2 teaspoons fruit spread down the inside center of each roll, starting near unrolled portion and ending 2 to 3 inches before the end of strip. Reroll the rolls to where the fruit spread stops. Using a sharp knife or scissors, cut each remaining part of dough strip without fruit spread lengthwise in half. Place rolls on cookie sheet, bending cut strips in half and arranging to create bunny ears.

3 Bake 16 to 18 minutes or until golden brown. Remove rolls from cookie sheet. Cool 5 minutes.

4 In small bowl, stir cream cheese and icing packet until almost smooth; stir in milk. Frost the top of rolls and ears. For each roll, place 2 raisins for eyes, a dollop of the reserved fruit spread for the nose, and peel-apart pieces for the whiskers.

> **Easy Cooking Tip** If you leave 2 inches of unrolled dough portions, they will be one-piece ears. Five-inch portions of unrolled dough will make two-piece ears when folded in half. Different types of ears and bending them in different ways before baking will give each bunny its own personality.

1 Roll Calories 420; Total Fat 15g (Saturated Fat 7g, Trans Fat 0g); Cholesterol 10mg; Sodium 790mg; Total Carbohydrate 66g (Dietary Fiber 2g); Protein 5g **Carbohydrate Choices:** 4½

Who wouldn't love a breakfast bake that tastes like cinnamon rolls? For a nutty flavor, top the baked breakfast casserole with ¼ cup toasted sliced almonds.

5-Ingredient Raspberry–Cream Cheese Cinnamon Roll Bake

PREP TIME: 15 Minutes • **START TO FINISH:** 55 Minutes • 8 servings

1 package (8 oz) cream cheese, softened

½ cup powdered sugar

1 teaspoon lemon zest

1 can (17.5 oz) refrigerated Annie's organic cinnamon rolls with icing (5 count)

2 cups fresh raspberries

1 to 2 teaspoons fresh lemon juice

1 Heat oven to 350°F. Spray 13×9-inch (3-quart) baking dish with cooking spray.

2 In large bowl, stir 6 ounces of the cream cheese, the powdered sugar, and lemon zest until smooth and creamy.

3 Separate cinnamon roll dough into 5 rolls; set icing aside. Cut each roll into 6 pieces; gently stir into cream cheese mixture. Gently stir ½ cup of the raspberries into cream cheese mixture. Spoon evenly into baking dish (rolls will expand, filling gaps as they bake).

4 Bake 26 to 28 minutes or until dough is baked through in center and golden brown. Sprinkle with remaining 1½ cups raspberries. Cool 10 minutes.

5 In small bowl, stir icing and remaining 2 ounces cream cheese until smooth. Add lemon juice, 1 teaspoon at a time, until thin enough to drizzle. Drizzle over breakfast bake. Cut into 2 rows by 4 rows. Serve warm.

1 Serving Calories 350; Total Fat 17g (Saturated Fat 9g, Trans Fat 0g); Cholesterol 30mg; Sodium 560mg; Total Carbohydrate 46g (Dietary Fiber 3g); Protein 4g **Carbohydrate Choices:** 3

delish in a dish

Baked scrambled eggs hold together well in these sandwiches, making them easy to eat on the go! Change them up with any flavored or plain mayonnaise. These tasty sandwiches will be a day-brightener for anybunny.

Easy Breakfast Sandwiches

PREP TIME: 15 Minutes ● **START TO FINISH:** 1 Hour ● 8 sandwiches

1 can (16 oz) refrigerated Annie's organic flaky biscuits (8 count)

8 eggs

1 tablespoon milk

¼ teaspoon pepper

4 medium green onions, chopped (¼ cup)

½ cup drained roasted red pepper strips (from 16-oz jar)

3 tablespoons chipotle mayonnaise

8 slices (¾ ounce each) Colby-Monterey Jack cheese blend

8 slices Canadian bacon (from 5-oz package)

1 Heat oven to 350°F. Prepare biscuits as directed on can. Leave oven temperature at 350°F.

2 Meanwhile, spray 13×9-inch (3-quart) baking dish with cooking spray. Add eggs, milk, and pepper to the baking dish. Beat egg mixture with fork or whisk. Sprinkle with onions; arrange pepper strips randomly over egg mixture.

3 Bake egg mixture 12 to 17 minutes or until center is set. Let stand 5 minutes. Cut into 2 rows by 4 rows.

4 Split biscuits horizontally. Spread split sides with chipotle mayonnaise. On bottom of each biscuit, layer cheese slice and Canadian bacon slice. Place egg piece on top of Canadian bacon (folding in half, if desired); cover with biscuit tops. Serve immediately.

1 Sandwich Calories 410; Total Fat 23g (Saturated Fat 9g, Trans Fat 0g); Cholesterol 220mg; Sodium 1,090mg; Total Carbohydrate 30g (Dietary Fiber 0g); Protein 20g **Carbohydrate Choices:** 2

It's a snap! Purchase a container of already cut-up mixed fruit from the produce section of your grocery store to top these day-starter pizzas, and breakfast is ready to be devoured.

Granola Breakfast Pizzas

PREP TIME: 20 Minutes • **START TO FINISH:** 30 Minutes • 4 pizzas

1 box (4.9 oz) Annie's Gluten Free Double Chocolate Chip or Oatmeal Cookie chewy granola bars (5 bars)

1 tablespoon plus 2 teaspoons honey

½ cup plain cream cheese spread (from 8-oz container)

¼ cup nonfat Greek vanilla yogurt

2 tablespoons apple carrot fruit purée (from 3.17-oz pouch)

1 cup assorted fresh fruit, cut into small pieces

1 Heat oven to 350°F. Line cookie sheet with cooking parchment paper; spray with cooking spray.

2 In medium bowl, crumble granola bars. Add 1 tablespoon and 1 teaspoon of the honey; mix with hands until granola is evenly coated (mixture will be sticky). Divide mixture into fourths; place at least 3½ inches apart on cookie sheet. Shape into 3-inch rounds.

3 Bake 5 to 6 minutes or until bubbly and golden brown. Cool completely, about 20 minutes. Carefully peel rounds from parchment.

4 Meanwhile, in small bowl, mix cream cheese and yogurt until blended. Stir in fruit purée.

5 Spoon cream cheese mixture evenly over each round. Toss fruit with remaining 1 teaspoon honey; spoon over cream cheese mixture. Serve immediately.

1 Pizza Calories 290; Total Fat 14g (Saturated Fat 8g, Trans Fat 0g); Cholesterol 30mg; Sodium 150mg; Total Carbohydrate 37g (Dietary Fiber 4g); Protein 5g **Carbohydrate Choices:** 2½

Cooking Gluten Free? Always read labels to make sure each recipe ingredient is gluten free. Products and ingredient sources can change.

Wake up your taste buds with a few Annie's organic chocolate Bunny Grahams on top of these sunshiny smoothie bowls. No frozen banana on hand? Use a room temperature banana for a smoothie bowl that's slightly less thick.

Ultimate Breakfast Smoothie Bowls

PREP TIME: 10 Minutes ● **START TO FINISH:** 10 Minutes ● 2 servings

1½ cups nonfat Greek vanilla yogurt

1 ripe medium banana, frozen, peeled, and cut into chunks

2 Annie's Gluten Free Double Chocolate Chip chewy granola bars (from 5.34-oz box)

½ cup fresh blueberries

½ cup fresh raspberries

2 tablespoons peanut butter or almond butter

1 In blender, place yogurt and banana chunks. Cover; blend on high speed 30 to 60 seconds or until smooth. Pour into 2 serving bowls.

2 Crumble 1 granola bar over each bowl; top with blueberries and raspberries. In small microwavable bowl, place peanut butter. Microwave uncovered on High about 10 seconds or until melted. Stir until smooth. Drizzle peanut butter over each serving. Serve immediately.

Easy Cooking Tip When your bananas are getting too ripe to eat, throw them in the freezer for easy smoothies anytime! Simply put the unpeeled bananas in a freezer storage bag. To use, microwave a frozen banana for about 1 minute on Medium-Low (30%) or just until it's easy to peel. Smoothies made with frozen bananas will be thicker and colder than those made with room temperature bananas.

1 Serving Calories 460; Total Fat 12g (Saturated Fat 3.5g, Trans Fat 0g); Cholesterol 10mg; Sodium 170mg; Total Carbohydrate 64g (Dietary Fiber 9g); Protein 21g **Carbohydrate Choices:** 4

A yummy breakfast or snack ya can eat with your fingers. If you like, use a cookie cutter that's about 1 inch wide or wider and 1 inch tall to cut the poppers into fun shapes. You'll get about 18 poppers plus scraps if you cut them this way.

Smoothie Poppers

PREP TIME: 10 Minutes • **START TO FINISH:** 4 Hours 10 Minutes • 24 poppers

	LIME GREEN SMOOTHIE POPPERS	**CARROT-MANGO SMOOTHIE POPPERS**	**BLUEBERRY-GRAPE SMOOTHIE POPPERS**
GELATIN + COLD JUICE	2 envelopes gelatin + ½ cup chilled apple juice	2 envelopes gelatin + ¼ cup chilled carrot juice	2 envelopes gelatin + ½ cup chilled Concord grape juice
BLENDER INGREDIENTS	2 containers (5.3 oz each) dairy-free Key lime yogurt alternative + ½ cup packed fresh baby spinach leaves	1⅓ cups dairy-free vanilla yogurt alternative (from a 24-oz container) + ½ cup chopped ripe mango	1⅓ cups dairy-free vanilla yogurt alternative (from a 24-oz container) + ½ cup fresh blueberries
JUICE, HEATED BOILING	¾ cup apple juice	¾ cup apple juice	¾ cup Concord grape juice

1 Lightly spray 9×5-inch loaf pan with cooking spray; blot with paper towel. Set aside.

2 In large bowl, sprinkle gelatin on cold juice to soften; let stand 1 minute. Meanwhile, in blender, place blender ingredients. Cover; blend on high speed until smooth.

3 Add hot juice to gelatin mixture; stir about 2 minutes or until gelatin is dissolved. Stir in yogurt mixture. Pour into loaf pan. Cover; refrigerate until firm, about 4 hours.

4 Cut into cubes and serve or cover and refrigerate up to 2 days before serving.

1 Lime Green Smoothie Popper Calories 20; Total Fat 0g (Saturated Fat 0g, Trans Fat 0g); Cholesterol 0mg; Sodium 0mg; Total Carbohydrate 3g (Dietary Fiber 0g); Protein 0g **Carbohydrate Choices:** 0

photo on next page

Look for Organic

When you buy food from the store, an easy way to know that the food is grown on organic farms is to look for the word "organic" and the USDA Organic seal. Unlike other words on labels, like "natural" or "sustainable," the word "organic" is strictly regulated by the US government to make sure that the food labeled that way came from certified farms that worked with nature and used methods that protect people and the planet.

FARM TO FORK STORY

Lime Green
Smoothie
Poppers

Blueberry-Grape
Smoothie Poppers

Carrot-Mango
Smoothie Poppers

No, you're not dreaming . . . you can eat mac for breakfast. Breakfast sausage, veggies, and eggs bring it into the daylight in this yummy baked dish.

Skillet Breakfast Mac & Cheese Bake

PREP TIME: 25 Minutes ● **START TO FINISH:** 50 Minutes ● 6 servings

2 boxes (6 oz each) Annie's Shells & Real Aged Cheddar macaroni & cheese

4 medium green onions, sliced (¼ cup)

2 tablespoons butter

½ lb bulk pork sausage

1 medium red bell pepper, chopped (1 cup)

½ cup milk

⅓ cup shredded sharp cheddar cheese

¼ cup plain panko crispy bread crumbs

6 eggs

Salt and pepper, if desired

1 Heat oven to 350°F. In 4-quart saucepan, heat 3 quarts (12 cups) water to boiling. Add pasta from boxes. Cook 7 to 9 minutes or until just tender; drain.

2 Meanwhile, reserve 1 tablespoon of green onions. In 12-inch ovenproof skillet, heat 1 tablespoon of butter over medium-high heat until melted. Add sausage, bell pepper, and remaining green onions. Cook, stirring occasionally, 5 to 7 minutes or until sausage is no longer pink and vegetables are tender. Remove from heat. Stir powdered cheese packets from boxes and milk into sausage mixture; stir in pasta. Set aside.

3 In small microwavable bowl, place remaining 1 tablespoon butter. Microwave uncovered on High about 30 seconds or until melted. Stir in cheese and bread crumbs. Set aside.

recipe continues

4 With back of spoon, make 6 (3-inch-wide) indentations in macaroni and cheese mixture. Break eggs, one at a time, into custard cup or small glass bowl; carefully slide egg into each indentation. Sprinkle eggs with salt and pepper. Sprinkle bread crumb mixture around eggs in skillet.

5 Bake uncovered 20 to 25 minutes or until whites are firm but yolks are still slightly runny. Bake longer for firm yolks, if desired. Sprinkle with reserved green onions.

1 Serving Calories 450; Total Fat 21g (Saturated Fat 9g, Trans Fat 0g); Cholesterol 230mg; Sodium 710mg; Total Carbohydrate 46g (Dietary Fiber 3g); Protein 20g **Carbohydrate Choices:** 3

That's Bananas!

Did you know that bananas are one of the most popular foods in the world? They mostly grow in tropical places, including Africa, Asia, and Central and South America. Banana plants are often called trees, but they are really a large herb, with a stalk that just looks like a tree trunk. A banana plant takes about nine months to grow, and each plant can grow more than 200 bananas! That's a lot of bananas!

World of Wheat

Did you know wheat is turned into flour, which is the main ingredient in bread, pasta, tortillas, cookies, crackers, and cakes? Wheat is grown all over the world, and after it's harvested, the wheat kernels get ground into flour. Wheat is sold by the bushel, and one bushel of wheat typically contains around 100,000,000 individual wheat kernels. That's enough wheat for 90 one-pound loaves of whole wheat bread!

Shareable Snacks

These playful pops are best enjoyed the same day they're made, but if you need to, they can be stored up to 24 hours.

Frozen Cocoa Bunny-Banana Pops

PREP TIME: 15 Minutes ● **START TO FINISH:** 2 Hours 15 Minutes ●
6 banana pops

3 ripe, firm medium bananas
6 wooden craft sticks
½ cup nonfat Greek vanilla yogurt
1½ teaspoons unsweetened baking cocoa

1½ teaspoons honey
1¾ cups Annie's organic Cocoa Bunnies or Cinna Bunnies cereal
1 tablespoon candy sprinkles

1 Line 15×10×1-inch pan with cooking parchment paper. Peel bananas; cut each in half crosswise. Insert craft stick into cut side of each banana half; place in pan. Freeze uncovered at least 1 hour.

2 In small bowl, mix yogurt, cocoa, and honey until well blended. Spoon and spread yogurt mixture over frozen banana halves, covering evenly. Gently press cereal onto banana pops; place in pan. Sprinkle both sides of pops with candy sprinkles.

3 Freeze uncovered about 1 hour or until yogurt is firm.

1 Banana Pop Calories 130; Total Fat 1.5g (Saturated Fat 0.5g, Trans Fat 0g); Cholesterol 0mg; Sodium 55mg; Total Carbohydrate 27g (Dietary Fiber 2g); Protein 3g **Carbohydrate Choices:** 2

Farms of All Sizes

Farms can range in size. There are small farms that grow enough food for a family or community, and large farms with thousands of acres that grow crops to sell to grocery stores and food companies to use as ingredients for food products.

A graham cracker base means the yogurt bark won't melt in your hands, the way typical yogurt bark does. Win!

Strawberry-Lemon Frozen Yogurt Bark

PREP TIME: 20 Minutes • **START TO FINISH:** 4 Hours 20 Minutes • 12 servings

13 honey graham cracker rectangles (from 14.4-oz box)

3 cups nonfat Greek vanilla yogurt

1 tablespoon lemon zest

2 tablespoons fresh lemon juice

2 tablespoons honey

1¾ cups sliced fresh strawberries

1½ teaspoons candy sprinkles

1 Line 15×10×1-inch pan with cooking parchment paper. Arrange graham crackers in pan, cutting 1 cracker in half lengthwise, to completely cover bottom of pan.

2 In medium bowl, mix yogurt, lemon zest, lemon juice, and honey until well blended. Spread evenly over graham crackers. Top yogurt mixture with strawberries and candy sprinkles.

3 Freeze uncovered about 4 hours until yogurt is firmly set.

4 Remove from freezer. Lift bark with parchment paper out of pan; loosen parchment paper from bark. Break into about 3-inch pieces. Let stand 3 to 5 minutes before serving. Serve immediately or store in covered container in freezer up to 24 hours.

1 Serving Calories 140; Total Fat 2g (Saturated Fat 0g, Trans Fat 0g); Cholesterol 0mg; Sodium 100mg; Total Carbohydrate 23g (Dietary Fiber 1g); Protein 6g **Carbohydrate Choices:** 1½

fruity-licious

So quick and easy as a snack . . . but these could also double as a breakfast or even a dessert. Any way ya serve them, they're going to disappear quickly.

Apple Nachos

PREP TIME: 10 Minutes ● **START TO FINISH:** 10 Minutes ● 4 servings

2 medium unpeeled or peeled Granny Smith apples, cut into quarters

3 tablespoons almond butter or peanut butter

2 tablespoons honey

½ cup sliced fresh strawberries

¼ cup Annie's organic Cinna Bunnies cereal

1 tablespoon miniature semisweet chocolate chips

1 Cut each apple quarter into 4 slices; arrange slices on serving platter or divide among 4 serving plates.

2 In small microwavable bowl, stir almond butter and honey until blended. Microwave uncovered on High 10 to 15 seconds or until softened; stir. Stir in 1 to 2 teaspoons water, if necessary, until thin enough to drizzle. Drizzle almond butter mixture evenly over apple slices. Sprinkle with strawberries, cereal, and chocolate chips. Serve immediately.

1 Serving Calories 200; Total Fat 8g (Saturated Fat 1.5g, Trans Fat 0g); Cholesterol 0mg; Sodium 40mg; Total Carbohydrate 29g (Dietary Fiber 4g); Protein 3g **Carbohydrate Choices:** 2

Cooking Vegetarian? Always read labels to make sure each recipe ingredient is vegetarian. Products and ingredient sources can change.

Make it easy to serve this hoppy snack! Whip up the Creamy Feta Dip and the herb mixture in Step 3 ahead of time. Cover and refrigerate the dip and let the herb mixture stand at room temperature until serving time.

Mediterranean Watermelon Fries with Creamy Feta Dip

PREP TIME: 10 Minutes • **START TO FINISH:** 10 Minutes • 5 servings (1 cup watermelon sticks and ¼ cup dip each)

Creamy Feta Dip

¼ cup crumbled feta cheese (1 oz)

1 container (6 oz) nonfat Greek plain yogurt

⅓ cup finely chopped cucumber

2 tablespoons milk

1 tablespoon chopped fresh mint leaves

Watermelon Fries

5 cups (3×½×½-inch) watermelon strips (about ¼ small melon)

½ teaspoon dried oregano leaves

¼ teaspoon salt

¼ teaspoon garlic powder

¼ teaspoon coarsely ground pepper

1 In small bowl, mash feta cheese with fork to break up large crumbles. Stir in remaining dip ingredients. Cover and refrigerate until ready to serve.

2 Arrange watermelon strips on platter.

3 In small bowl, stir together oregano, salt, garlic powder, and pepper. Sprinkle oregano mixture evenly over watermelon. Serve with dip.

1 Serving Calories 100; Total Fat 2.5g (Saturated Fat 1.5g, Trans Fat 0g); Cholesterol 10mg; Sodium 200mg; Total Carbohydrate 14g (Dietary Fiber 0g); Protein 5g **Carbohydrate Choices:** 1

Cooking without Nut Ingredients? Always read labels to make sure each ingredient is made without nuts. Products, ingredients, and processing methods can change.
Cooking Gluten Free? Always read labels to make sure each recipe ingredient is gluten free. Products and ingredient sources can change.

A snack ya can play with! A thick peanut butter works best to hold these cute snacks together. If using natural peanut butter, mix it well before measuring.

Peanut Butter Graham Spinners

PREP TIME: 20 Minutes • **START TO FINISH:** 20 Minutes • 4 spinners

3 pouches Annie's organic Bees, Bugs & Butterflies fruit snacks (from 4-oz box)

16 pretzel sticks (from 8-oz package)

¼ cup plus 2 teaspoons creamy peanut butter or almond butter

4 honey graham cracker rectangles, cut crosswise in half

4 Annie's organic Chocolate Bunny Grahams (from 7.5-oz box)

1 Gently press 1 fruit snack piece onto one end of each pretzel piece.

2 Spread ¼ cup of the peanut butter on bottom sides of crackers. Press 4 pretzel pieces each onto 4 of the crackers, fruit snack end out, in a spoke fashion. Top with remaining crackers, peanut butter side down. Press each spinner lightly together.

3 Spread ½ teaspoon of remaining peanut butter onto the top of each spinner; press additional fruit snacks and the bunny crackers into the peanut butter.

1 Spinner Calories 260; Total Fat 11g (Saturated Fat 2g, Trans Fat 0g); Cholesterol 0mg; Sodium 240mg; Total Carbohydrate 33g (Dietary Fiber 1g); Protein 5g **Carbohydrate Choices:** 2

Keep individual serving-size bags of this tasty mix stashed in the car or your purse for when the kiddos' tummy clocks click over to empty.

Sweet ● Salty Snack Mix

PREP TIME: 10 Minutes ● **START TO FINISH:** 10 Minutes ● 6 servings (about 1 cup each)

2 cups popped popcorn

1 cup Annie's organic Birthday Cake cereal

1 cup Annie's organic White Cheddar Bunnies (from 7.5-oz box)

1 cup yogurt-covered raisins or ½ cup raisins

1 cup pretzel twists

½ cup roasted, salted almonds

1 box (4 oz) Annie's organic Summer Strawberry Bunny fruit snacks (5 pouches)

In large bowl, mix all ingredients. Store tightly covered at room temperature up to 7 days.

1 Serving Calories 390; Total Fat 15g (Saturated Fat 6g, Trans Fat 0g); Cholesterol 0mg; Sodium 280mg; Total Carbohydrate 57g (Dietary Fiber 3g); Protein 5g **Carbohydrate Choices:** 4

Poultry Farms

Poultry farms are farms that raise birds for their meat or eggs. These birds can be chickens, turkeys, or ducks. Did you know that chickens raised for their meat are usually a different breed than chickens that are raised for eggs? Chickens that lay eggs are called laying hens. On organic farms, the laying hens are never kept in small cages and can go outside. They eat organic feed and are never given antibiotics.

Allowing the cereal mixture to cool before adding the other ingredients keeps them from getting coated with the cinnamon mixture, so ya can identify all the shapes and colors of this happy snack mix.

Cinna Bunnies–Muddy Buddy Mix

PREP TIME: 15 Minutes ● **START TO FINISH:** 35 Minutes ● 14 servings (½ cup each)

3 cups Annie's organic Cinna Bunnies cinnamon cereal

¾ cup powdered sugar

½ teaspoon ground cinnamon

1½ bars (3.5 or 4.4 oz each) white chocolate, chopped

1 cup gluten-free pretzel twists or sticks

1 package (1.2 oz) freeze-dried strawberries

4 pouches Annie's organic Summer Strawberry fruit snacks (from 4-oz box)

1 In large microwavable bowl, place cereal; set aside. In 1-gallon resealable food-storage plastic bag, place powdered sugar and cinnamon; seal bag. Shake bag until mixed; set aside.

2 In medium microwavable bowl, microwave white chocolate uncovered on Medium-High (70%) 1 minute; stir. Microwave 30 seconds to 1 minute, stirring every 15 seconds, until chocolate is melted and can be stirred smooth.

3 Pour melted chocolate over cereal in bowl; stir until well coated. Add coated cereal to powdered sugar mixture in bag; seal bag. Shake until cereal is well coated. Spread on waxed paper to cool, about 20 minutes.

4 In large bowl, toss cereal mixture with pretzels and strawberries. Top with fruit snacks. Store loosely covered up to 5 days.

1 Serving Calories 140; Total Fat 3.5g (Saturated Fat 2.5g, Trans Fat 0g); Cholesterol 0mg; Sodium 100mg; Total Carbohydrate 28g (Dietary Fiber 0g); Protein 1g **Carbohydrate Choices:** 2

Cooking Gluten Free? Always read labels to make sure each recipe ingredient is gluten free. Products and ingredient sources can change.

Add a little joy to the day with this sweet and salty snack mix. Change up the sprinkles to fit the season or occasion for a surprise every time ya make it. This mix is best the day it's made. If needed, store loosely covered at room temperature for up to 2 days.

Cobweb Crunch Mix

PREP TIME: 10 Minutes • **START TO FINISH:** 40 Minutes • 5 servings (about 1 cup each)

1 cup mini pretzel twists
½ cup white vanilla baking chips
5 teaspoons black and orange sprinkles or nonpareils
2 cups popped popcorn

1 cup Annie's organic Honey Bunny Grahams (from 7.5-oz box)
1 box (4 oz) Annie's organic Berry Patch or Summer Strawberry Bunny fruit snacks (5 pouches)

1 Line 15×10×1-inch pan with waxed paper; spread pretzels evenly in pan.

2 In medium microwavable bowl, microwave white vanilla baking chips uncovered on Medium (50%) 45 seconds; stir. Microwave 30 seconds to 1 minute, stirring every 15 seconds, until chocolate is melted and can be stirred smooth.

3 Spoon baking chips into 1-pint resealable food-storage plastic bag. Snip small corner from one end. Drizzle onto pretzels to resemble cobwebs; immediately sprinkle with sprinkles. Let stand about 30 minutes or until set.

4 In large bowl, place popcorn, grahams, and fruit snacks; mix. Stir in pretzels.

1 Serving Calories 280; Total Fat 9g (Saturated Fat 4g, Trans Fat 0g); Cholesterol 0mg; Sodium 270mg; Total Carbohydrate 49g (Dietary Fiber 0g); Protein 3g **Carbohydrate Choices:** 3

Joyful Surprise Bento Boxes

What would bring a midday smile? How about a surprise lunch that reminds them you're thinking about them! A meal filled with goodness and fun all rolled up in one. The afternoon will look a little easier with a little love at noon.

Bento Boxes

Bento boxes are popular for lunch boxes or snacks, as the individual compartments keep foods separate and safe during travels. Bento boxes come with varying numbers and shapes of compartments, depending on your preference. Look for one with three or four compartments, to hold a nice variety of food types with interesting colors and textures.

Get Creative

Why have a simple sandwich, veggie sticks, and fruit when lunch could have a theme such as bugs, dinosaurs, or everything-stars? Use your calendar or imagination for themes. How about a patriotic red, white, and blue lunch or everything green for St. Patrick's Day? Bread cutters and cookie cutters can cut sandwiches, fruit and veggies, and even cheese into shapes to fit your theme. No time for an entirely themed meal? Make just one compartment something fun and unexpected for a surprise and delight.

Choosing Food

Aim for foods that add up to be a complete meal (protein, carbs, fruit, and veggies), with a variety of colors, textures, and shapes so lunch is never boring. If peanut butter and jelly is the only thing they'll eat, try cutting the sandwiches into flowers or other shapes with cookie cutters. Fruit and veggies can be fun on their own or made into adorable animals or bugs. And don't discount the value of edible googly eyes that can turn any food into a face!

Add a Note

Let them know you're thinking of them by adding a note to the lunch. Just a quick sentence or two of encouragement or an "I believe in YOU" is the dot on the exclamation point to a joyful meal.

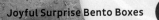

fun in
a glass

Add other fruit, such as strawberries, pineapple chunks, blueberries, kiwi chunks, and grapes, to the skewers. Double the fruit and fun with a second skewer. No bunny can resist these over-the-top shakes brimming with fruity goodness.

Watermelon Birthday Cake Shakes

PREP TIME: 15 Minutes • **START TO FINISH:** 15 Minutes • 2 shakes

Fruit Skewers
1 slice seedless watermelon, 1 inch thick

2 (10-inch) wooden skewers

Shakes
2½ cups vanilla frozen yogurt

1½ cups Annie's organic Birthday Cake cereal

½ cup orange juice

Additional bite-size pieces of fruit for skewers and glasses, if desired

1 Using 2-inch cookie cutter, cut 4 shapes out of watermelon slice. Trim rind away from watermelon slice; cut remaining watermelon into 1-inch pieces; measure 1 cup; set aside. Reserve any remaining watermelon for another use. Thread watermelon shapes and additional fruit onto top half of each wooden skewer; set aside.

2 In blender, place frozen yogurt, 1 cup of the cereal, the orange juice, and reserved watermelon pieces. Cover; blend on high speed, stopping occasionally and scraping down sides with rubber spatula, 1 to 2 minutes or until smooth. Pour into 2 tall glasses. Top shakes with remaining cereal. Insert skewer into each glass. Add additional fruit to rim of each glass. Serve immediately.

1 Shake Calories 400; Total Fat 4g (Saturated Fat 2g, Trans Fat 0g); Cholesterol 15mg; Sodium 170mg; Total Carbohydrate 82g (Dietary Fiber 1g); Protein 10g **Carbohydrate Choices:** 5½

The chocolatey fruitiness of these shakes makes a delicious breakfast on the go. When bananas get overripe, throw them whole in the freezer for shakes or smoothies. See page 43 for how to freeze bananas and peel them once they're frozen.

Chocolate-Banana Bunny Shakes

PREP TIME: 5 Minutes ● **START TO FINISH:** 5 Minutes ● 2 shakes

2 ripe medium bananas, frozen
1 cup chocolate milk
½ cup Annie's organic Cocoa Bunnies cereal
½ cup chopped fresh strawberries

Additional Annie's organic Cocoa Bunnies cereal, if desired
2 small whole fresh strawberries, if desired

1 Microwave frozen bananas about 1 minute on Medium-Low (30%) or just until easy enough to peel. Peel; cut into chunks.

2 In blender, place bananas, chocolate milk, and ½ cup of the cereal. Cover; blend on high speed about 30 seconds or until smooth. Stir in ½ cup chopped strawberries.

3 Pour into 2 glasses. Top shakes with additional cereal; garnish each glass with 1 strawberry.

1 Shake Calories 260; Total Fat 3.5g (Saturated Fat 1.5g, Trans Fat 0g); Cholesterol 10mg; Sodium 125mg; Total Carbohydrate 52g (Dietary Fiber 5g); Protein 6g **Carbohydrate Choices:** 3½

Cleaning the blender will be easy! After pouring the smoothies into glasses, fill the blender halfway with water. Cover and pulse a few times to loosen any stuck-on food.

Blueberry-Peach Smoothies

PREP TIME: 5 Minutes ● **START TO FINISH:** 5 Minutes ● 2 servings

1½ cups unsweetened almond milk

1 container (5.3 oz) fat-free Greek peach yogurt

2 cups frozen sliced peaches

½ cup frozen blueberries

Additional frozen blueberries, if desired

1 In blender, place all ingredients except additional frozen blueberries. Cover; blend on high speed about 1 minute or until smooth, scraping down sides of blender as needed.

2 Pour into 2 glasses. Sprinkle with additional frozen blueberries. Serve immediately.

1 Serving Calories 190; Total Fat 2.5g (Saturated Fat 0g, Trans Fat 0g); Cholesterol 0mg; Sodium 160mg; Total Carbohydrate 33g (Dietary Fiber 5g); Protein 8g **Carbohydrate Choices:** 2

Cooking Gluten Free? Always read labels to make sure each recipe ingredient is gluten free. Products and ingredient sources can change.

Dairy Farms

Milk, cheese, yogurt, and ice cream are all milk products that start on dairy farms. Mostly cows but also sheep and goats can be raised to provide milk for drinking and other milk-based foods. On organic farms, cows are raised on pastures, where they can eat grasses and other plants like clover. That makes the cows happy! It also means that the milk they produce is better for you.

If your blender leaves frozen fruit a little lumpy, thaw the mango chunks about 30 seconds in the microwave first.

Mango Green Smoothies

PREP TIME: 5 Minutes ● **START TO FINISH:** 5 Minutes ● 2 servings

1½ cups unsweetened almond milk

1 container (5.3 oz) nonfat Greek plain yogurt

2 cups packed fresh baby spinach leaves

2 cups frozen mango chunks

1 In blender, place all ingredients. Cover; blend on high speed 1 to 2 minutes or until smooth, scraping down sides of blender as needed.

2 Pour into 2 glasses. Serve immediately.

1 Serving Calories 200; Total Fat 4g (Saturated Fat 1g, Trans Fat 0g); Cholesterol 10mg; Sodium 170mg; Total Carbohydrate 28g (Dietary Fiber 3g); Protein 11g **Carbohydrate Choices:** 2

Cooking Gluten Free? Always read labels to make sure each recipe ingredient is gluten free. Products and ingredient sources can change.

What Is a Ranch?

A ranch is a farm that raises animals such as beef cows or horses. There are even ranches that raise alpacas, emu, bison, or elk. Ranches let their animals eat plants that grow on the range, and they may also raise additional crops for feeding their animals, especially in winter. If you'd like to try being a rancher, you can visit a working ranch, known as a dude ranch, where they let you help with the daily farm jobs, possibly including horseback riding to drive cattle across the wide-open range. Yee-haw!

You can prepare frozen bananas as directed below or, to quickly freeze one that's on your counter, line a small plate with waxed paper. Cut the banana crosswise into slices, place on single layer on plate, and freeze uncovered about 1 hour.

Lava Smoothies

PREP TIME: 10 Minutes ● **START TO FINISH:** 1 Hour 10 Minutes ●
2 servings

1 ripe medium banana, frozen

¾ cup refrigerated organic mango juice blend or carrot-citrus juice blend (from 15.2-oz bottle)

1 container (5.3 oz) nut- and dairy-free vanilla yogurt alternative

1 cup ice cubes

¾ cup dark red 100% juice (such as beet, carrot, and orange), chilled (from 32-oz bottle)

1 tablespoon agave nectar

1 Microwave frozen banana about 1 minute on Medium-Low (30%) or just until easy enough to peel. Peel; cut into quarters.

2 In blender, place mango juice blend, half of the banana, half of the yogurt, and half of the ice. Cover; blend on medium speed 30 seconds or until smooth. Pour into 2-cup measure, scraping sides of blender container. Rinse blender container and lid.

3 In same blender container, place beet juice blend, agave nectar, and remaining banana, yogurt, and ice. Cover; blend on medium speed 30 seconds or until smooth.

4 For each smoothie, tilt 12-ounce glass. Pour half the orange smoothie into glass. With glass still tilted, pour half of the red smoothie on top of the orange smoothie; straighten glass. Serve immediately.

1 Serving Calories 220; Total Fat 2g (Saturated Fat 0g, Trans Fat 0g); Cholesterol 0mg; Sodium 85mg; Total Carbohydrate 46g (Dietary Fiber 4g); Protein 4g **Carbohydrate Choices:** 3

Cooking without Dairy or Nut Ingredients? Always read labels to make sure each ingredient is made without dairy or nuts. Products, ingredients, and processing methods can change.

Cooking Vegetarian or Vegan? Always read labels to make sure each recipe ingredient is vegetarian or vegan. Products and ingredient sources can change.

crispy and
cheesy

Mac ya can eat with your fingers! For even more fun flavor, serve up warm marinara sauce or ketchup for dipping.

Mac & Double Cheese Sticks

PREP TIME: 30 Minutes ● **START TO FINISH:** 3 Hours 45 Minutes ●
4 servings (3 sticks each)

Mac & Cheese

1 box (6 oz) Annie's Shells & Real Aged Cheddar macaroni & cheese

3 tablespoons milk

1 cup shredded Colby–Monterey Jack cheese blend (4 oz)

1 egg, beaten

½ cup fresh basil leaves, chopped

Breading

⅓ cup all-purpose flour

3 eggs, beaten

2 cups plain panko crispy bread crumbs

1 In 3-quart saucepan, heat 6 cups water to boiling over high heat. Add pasta from box. Heat to boiling; reduce heat. Simmer uncovered 9 to 11 minutes or until very tender; drain. Return pasta to pan. Stir in milk, powdered cheese packet from box, and Colby–Monterey Jack cheese. Let stand uncovered 5 minutes. Stir in 1 egg and basil leaves.

2 Line 8-inch square baking pan with foil, leaving 2-inch overhang on two opposite sides of pan for easy removal; spray with cooking spray. Spread mac & cheese in even layer in pan; flatten top with spatula. Cover with plastic wrap. Freeze until frozen, at least 3 hours or overnight.

3 Heat oven to 425°F. Line 15×10×1-inch rectangular baking pan with cooking parchment paper.

4 Lift frozen pasta mixture out of pan with foil; pull back foil from edges. Using sharp knife, cut pasta mixture into 2 rows by 6 rows. In shallow bowl or pie plate, place flour. In another shallow bowl or pie

recipe continues

plate, place remaining eggs. In third shallow bowl or pie plate, place bread crumbs. Dip each stick in flour mixture, then dip in eggs. Coat well with bread crumbs; shake off excess. Place on pan, leaving space between pieces.

5 Bake 12 to 15 minutes or until golden brown and sticks are hot in center.

1 Serving Calories 600; Total Fat 20g (Saturated Fat 10g, Trans Fat 0g); Cholesterol 220mg; Sodium 930mg; Total Carbohydrate 78g (Dietary Fiber 4g); Protein 27g **Carbohydrate Choices:** 5

What Jobs Are Done on a Farm?

Crop farmers need to prepare and maintain the land for growing plants, protect their crops from disease and pests, and help the plants grow. The crops are grown from seeds, watered if there isn't enough rain, and picked or harvested when fully grown.

Ranchers and *dairy and poultry farmers* take care of the animals daily by feeding them, making sure they have water, keeping the spaces where they live clean, and more so they grow and remain strong and healthy. Farmers also take care of any repairs needed to fences, buildings, and farm tools so the farm keeps running smoothly.

Organic Farming

Organic farmers grow healthy crops without using chemicals like fertilizers or pesticides. They work in harmony with nature to create the right conditions on the farm for the crops to grow. These sustainable farming methods are better for people, the environment, and the planet. For example, to give the crops the nutrients they need to grow well, organic farmers build healthy soil that feeds the plants. To get rid of weeds in their fields or unwanted insects that eat their crops, organic farmers manage their farms in ways that prevent weeds and insects from becoming a problem in the first place. And if they do become a problem, organic farmers deal with them in ways that make it less likely that other living creatures will be harmed.

Serve with warm marinara sauce or ranch dressing—or both. Change up the flavor of these crunchy 2-bite snacks by using other varieties of cheese sticks. Yum!

Easy Baked Mozzarella Bites

PREP TIME: 20 Minutes • **START TO FINISH:** 35 Minutes • 24 bites

1 can (8 oz) refrigerated Annie's organic crescent rolls (8 rolls)

8 mozzarella sticks, unwrapped, cut crosswise into thirds (from 12-oz package)

3 tablespoons butter, melted

⅔ cup Italian-style panko crispy bread crumbs

1 Heat oven to 375°F. Unroll dough on cutting board; starting at center, press into 12×8-inch rectangle, pressing perforations to seal. Using pizza cutter or sharp knife, cut rectangle into 6 rows by 4 rows to make 24 (2-inch) squares.

2 Place mozzarella stick in center of each rectangle. Bring dough up and around cheese sticks; press edges to seal.

3 In small bowl, pour melted butter. In another small bowl, place bread crumbs. Dip each stick into butter; shake off excess. Roll in bread crumbs to coat. Place about 1 inch apart on ungreased large cookie sheet.

4 Bake 11 to 13 minutes or until golden brown. Serve warm.

1 Bite Calories 80; Total Fat 5g (Saturated Fat 2.5g, Trans Fat 0g); Cholesterol 10mg; Sodium 190mg; Total Carbohydrate 6g (Dietary Fiber 0g); Protein 2g **Carbohydrate Choices:** ½

Everybunny's going to dive into these yummy morsels. Like 'em really spicy? Vary the level of spiciness by using a different heat level of buffalo sauce.

Buffalo Chicken Bites

PREP TIME: 15 Minutes ● **START TO FINISH:** 30 Minutes ● 16 bites

1 can (8 oz) refrigerated Annie's organic crescent rolls (8 rolls)

½ cup diced cooked chicken

2 tablespoons crumbled blue cheese or shredded mozzarella cheese

2 tablespoons Buffalo wing sauce

2 oz cream cheese, softened (from 8-oz package)

1 medium green onion, chopped, if desired

1 Heat oven to 350°F. Unroll dough; cut rectangles lengthwise in half. On ungreased cookie sheet, place rectangles.

2 In small bowl, mix remaining ingredients. Spoon mixture on half of each rectangle; fold dough over filling. Press edges with fork to seal.

3 Bake 13 to 16 minutes or just until golden brown.

1 Bite Calories 70; Total Fat 4.5g (Saturated Fat 2g, Trans Fat 0g); Cholesterol 10mg; Sodium 190mg; Total Carbohydrate 6g (Dietary Fiber 0g); Protein 2g **Carbohydrate Choices:** ½

Orchards Are Also Farms

Some foods, like oats, wheat, and corn, are grown from seeds that the farmer plants in the soil. Other crops are grown on bushes, like raspberries and blueberries. And lots of fruits grow on trees. Farms that grow trees for fruit or nuts like apples, cherries, or almonds are known as orchards. Citrus fruit farms (that grow oranges or grapefruits) are known as groves. Many orchards are open to visitors, and sometimes you can pick your own fruit to take home. Yum!

This is one irresistible snackity-snack. Got regular-size hot dogs? Use 3, each cut crosswise into thirds, in place of the mini ones. Dunk them in ketchup, if sauce is your thing.

Cheesy Piglets in a Blanket

PREP TIME: 15 Minutes ● **START TO FINISH:** 30 Minutes ● 8 servings (3 pieces each)

1 can (8 oz) refrigerated Annie's organic crescent rolls (8 rolls)

6 slices (¾ oz each) cheddar cheese

24 miniature uncured hot dogs

1 Heat oven to 375°F. Line large cookie sheet with cooking parchment paper.

2 Unroll can of dough; separate into 8 triangles. Cut each triangle lengthwise into 3 narrow triangles. Cut each cheese slice into 4 strips.

3 Place cheese strip along length of each triangle. Place 1 miniature hot dog on top of cheese at base of shortest side of triangle. Roll up each triangle, starting at shortest side of triangle and rolling to opposite point; place point side down on cookie sheet.

4 Bake 12 to 15 minutes or until golden brown. Serve warm.

1 Serving Calories 250; Total Fat 18g (Saturated Fat 7g, Trans Fat 0g); Cholesterol 40mg; Sodium 650mg; Total Carbohydrate 14g (Dietary Fiber 0g); Protein 7g **Carbohydrate Choices:** 1

FARM TO FORK STORY

California Fruits and Nuts

The long, sunny days and mild weather of California make it ideal for growing two-thirds of the country's fruits and nuts. Almonds, grapes, pistachios, lettuce, strawberries, flowers, and walnuts are in the top 10 foods produced in California. What a yummy place to live!

Mini peppers come in different shapes and sizes. Use ones that are about 3 inches long and wide enough to be easily filled with the cheese mixture. If ya like, assemble them ahead of time and refrigerate. When you're ready to serve, pop them in the broiler and serve 'em up hot!

Herbed Goat Cheese Pizza Poppers

PREP TIME: 15 Minutes • **START TO FINISH:** 15 Minutes • 8 servings (2 halves each)

1 package (4 oz) plain goat cheese, softened

¾ cup shredded mozzarella cheese (3 oz)

1½ teaspoons chopped fresh thyme leaves

8 mini bell peppers, cut in half, seeded, stems intact

¼ cup gluten-free pizza sauce

1 Set oven to broil; position oven rack 6 inches from broiler. Line 15×10×1-inch pan with foil.

2 In medium bowl, place goat cheese, ¼ cup of the mozzarella cheese, and the thyme; mix well. Spoon mixture into pepper halves, dividing equally. Top peppers with remaining ½ cup mozzarella cheese, divided evenly. Place peppers in pan.

3 Broil for 1 to 1½ minutes or until cheese is melted and starting to brown.

4 Remove from oven; drizzle with pizza sauce. Serve immediately.

1 Serving Calories 100; Total Fat 7g (Saturated Fat 4g, Trans Fat 0g); Cholesterol 20mg; Sodium 160mg; Total Carbohydrate 4g (Dietary Fiber 1g); Protein 6g **Carbohydrate Choices:** 0

Cooking without Nut Ingredients? Always read labels to make sure each ingredient is made without nuts. Products, ingredients, and processing methods can change.
Cooking Gluten Free? Always read labels to make sure each recipe ingredient is gluten free. Products and ingredient sources can change.
Cooking Vegetarian? Always read labels to make sure each recipe ingredient is vegetarian. Products and ingredient sources can change.

Delicious Dinners Together

We have three words for this three-ingredient chicken recipe: *yum, yum, yum!* Serve it on its own, piled high as a sandwich on a bun with red onion slices, or any other way ya can think of. It seriously couldn't be any easier.

Three-Ingredient Sweet ● Spicy Pulled Chicken

PREP TIME: 10 Minutes ● **START TO FINISH:** 3 Hours 50 Minutes ●
8 servings

2½ lb boneless skinless chicken thighs

1 bottle (12 oz) sweet-and-spicy barbecue sauce (1½ cups)

2 tablespoons yellow mustard

1 Spray 4-quart slow cooker with cooking spray.

2 In slow cooker, mix chicken, ¼ cup of the barbecue sauce, and the mustard. Cover; cook on Low heat setting 3½ to 4 hours or until juice of chicken is clear when thickest part is cut (at least 165°F).

3 Remove chicken from slow cooker to medium bowl; discard cooking liquid. Using 2 forks, shred chicken; return chicken to slow cooker. Stir in remaining barbecue sauce; cover. Cook on High heat setting 10 to 15 minutes or until heated through.

1 Serving Calories 230; Total Fat 7g (Saturated Fat 2g, Trans Fat 0g); Cholesterol 135mg; Sodium 530mg; Total Carbohydrate 13g (Dietary Fiber 1g); Protein 29g **Carbohydrate Choices:** 1

Cooking without Dairy or Nut Ingredients? Always read labels to make sure each ingredient is made without dairy or nut ingredients. Products, ingredients, and processing methods can change.

No need to heat up the kitchen! These sandwiches are done completely on the grill. Offer your favorite toppings, such as sliced red onions, prepared guacamole, salsa, sliced peppers, or pico de gallo, and let everybunny top their own sandwich.

Grilled Mexican-Inspired Chicken Sandwiches

PREP TIME: 15 Minutes ● **START TO FINISH:** 45 Minutes ● 8 servings

4 (about 5 oz each) boneless skinless chicken breasts

1 package (1 oz) taco seasoning mix

8 slices (¾ oz each) pepper Jack cheese

1 can (16 oz) refrigerated Annie's organic flaky biscuits (8 count)

1 Heat gas or charcoal grill for indirect cooking over medium heat. Coat chicken breasts with taco seasoning mix; place on grill over heated portion.

2 Cover grill. Cook 12 to 15 minutes, turning once, until juice of chicken is clear when center of thickest part is cut (at least 165°F). Cut each chicken breast in half crosswise.

3 Top each chicken piece with cheese slice. Cook 1 minute longer or until cheese is melted. Move to unheated portion of grill; keep warm.

4 Separate dough into 8 biscuits. Place 18×12-inch double thickness of heavy-duty foil sprayed with cooking spray on grill, spray side up, over unheated portion. Place biscuits on foil, about 3 inches apart; cover. Cook 16 to 19 minutes or until golden brown.

5 Split biscuits in half. Place chicken on one half of each biscuit; top with remaining biscuit half.

1 Serving Calories 360; Total Fat 16g (Saturated Fat 7g, Trans Fat 0g); Cholesterol 70mg; Sodium 990mg; Total Carbohydrate 30g (Dietary Fiber 1g); Protein 26g **Carbohydrate Choices:** 2

Fun it up with your favorite flavored chicken sausage instead of the Italian chicken sausage in this delish dinner. A crusty loaf of French bread would make a nice dinner buddy for the mac.

Easy Chicken Sausage Mac

PREP TIME: 15 Minutes ● **START TO FINISH:** 20 Minutes ● 2 servings

1 box (6 oz) Annie's Macaroni & Classic Cheddar

3 tablespoons milk

2 tablespoons unsalted butter

2 fully cooked sweet Italian chicken sausages, coarsely chopped (from 12-oz package)

2 cups coarsely chopped spinach and kale blend

1 In 3-quart saucepan, prepare macaroni and cheese as directed on box, using milk and butter.

2 Meanwhile, in 10-inch nonstick skillet, cook sausage over medium-high heat 3 to 4 minutes, stirring occasionally, until heated through. Stir in spinach mixture. Cook over medium heat 2 to 3 minutes, stirring occasionally, until wilted.

3 Stir sausage and spinach mixture into pasta.

1 Serving Calories 580; Total Fat 24g (Saturated Fat 13g, Trans Fat 0g); Cholesterol 110mg; Sodium 1,140mg; Total Carbohydrate 62g (Dietary Fiber 3g); Protein 28g **Carbohydrate Choices:** 4

Start a School Garden

Ask your school if you can start a school garden! There are a number of school garden programs across the United States to tap into for tips on how to start one. Ask your parent or teachers to help research or even apply for a school garden grant. What fun to get your hands dirty, learn about plants, and taste-test different fruits and vegetables with your classmates!

**warm and
melty**

↓

The cheese cracker crumbs infuse cheesy-flavored goodness into these yummy chicken tenders! Crush them in a 1-gallon resealable food-storage plastic bag with a rolling pin or meat mallet, and ya can keep them in the bag for coating the chicken, cutting down on mess and dishes!

Cheddar Cracker Chicken Tenders

PREP TIME: 15 Minutes ● **START TO FINISH:** 35 Minutes ● 4 servings

2 eggs
2 cups Annie's organic Cheddar Bunnies, coarsely crushed (from 7.5-oz box)

1 package (14 oz) boneless skinless chicken breast tenders
¼ teaspoon salt
2 tablespoons butter, melted
Honey mustard, if desired

1 Heat oven to 425°F. Spray 15×10×1-inch pan with cooking spray.

2 In shallow bowl or pie plate, beat eggs. In another shallow bowl or pie plate, place cracker crumbs. Dip each chicken tender into eggs, then coat with cracker crumbs; place in pan. Sprinkle with salt; drizzle with melted butter.

3 Bake 12 to 18 minutes or until chicken is no longer pink in center. Serve with honey mustard.

> **Easy Cooking Tip** Cleanup is a breeze if you line the pan with foil before spraying with cooking spray.

1 Serving Calories 320; Total Fat 15g (Saturated Fat 5g, Trans Fat 0g); Cholesterol 150mg; Sodium 590mg; Total Carbohydrate 19g (Dietary Fiber 0g); Protein 27g **Carbohydrate Choices:** 1

What Is Biodiversity?

Did you know that all living things—animals (including people and insects), plants, and even creatures you can't see, like bacteria—need one another to thrive and survive? Biodiversity means the variety of living creatures, and we all rely on one another. For example, there are more than 100 crops grown in the United States that require pollinators like bees, butterflies, and other insects to grow. In fact, according to the National Parks Service, one out of every three bites of food you eat exists because of the efforts of pollinators. Without these creatures, we wouldn't have yummy foods like berries or nuts. Cool, huh? Biodiversity keeps ecosystems in balance and keeps our planet livable.

All the broccoli will come out perfectly cooked if ya start with pieces roughly the same size.

Parmesan Chicken Fingers ●and Roasted Veggies

PREP TIME: 15 Minutes ● **START TO FINISH:** 40 Minutes ● 4 servings

¾ lb small red potatoes, quartered

3 tablespoons olive oil

¾ teaspoon salt

¼ teaspoon seasoned pepper blend

2 cups fresh broccoli florets

1 clove garlic, finely chopped

⅓ cup Italian-style panko crispy bread crumbs

2 tablespoons all-purpose flour

2 tablespoons grated Parmesan cheese

1 egg

1 package (14 oz) boneless skinless chicken breast tenders

Chopped fresh Italian (flat-leaf) parsley, if desired

1 Heat oven to 450°F. Line 18×13-inch half-sheet pan with cooking parchment paper.

2 In medium bowl, mix potatoes, 1 tablespoon of the oil, ¼ teaspoon of the salt, and the seasoned pepper until well coated. Spoon potato mixture in a single layer on one-half of sheet pan.

3 Roast uncovered 8 minutes.

4 In same bowl, place broccoli, garlic, 1 tablespoon of the oil, and ¼ teaspoon of the salt; toss until coated. In large resealable food-storage plastic bag, mix bread crumbs, flour, Parmesan cheese, and remaining ¼ teaspoon salt. In small bowl, beat egg.

5 Dip chicken tenders in egg; place in bag with bread crumb mixture. Seal bag; shake to coat evenly. Place chicken tenders on other half of pan; drizzle with remaining 1 tablespoon oil. Stir broccoli mixture into potatoes on pan.

recipe continues

6 Roast uncovered 10 to 12 minutes or until chicken is no longer pink in center and potatoes are fork tender. Sprinkle with parsley.

1 Serving Calories 380; Total Fat 16g (Saturated Fat 3.5g, Trans Fat 0g); Cholesterol 110mg; Sodium 750mg; Total Carbohydrate 28g (Dietary Fiber 3g); Protein 29g **Carbohydrate Choices:** 2

Cooking without Nut Ingredients? Always read labels to make sure each ingredient is made without nuts. Products, ingredients, and processing methods can change.

Organic and Regenerative Agriculture

In order to feed everyone in the world with healthy foods for generations to come, farmers need a healthy planet with a stable climate, clean water, living soil, and biodiversity. Organic and regenerative farming focuses on working with nature to preserve and protect a healthy planet. That's why our food choices matter: When you buy organic food, you're supporting farmers who take good care of the soil and the water and protect biodiversity. We can all make a difference!

Orzo is a pasta that's shaped like rice but cooks in almost half the time. If ya can't find mozzarella cheese pearls, shredded mozzarella is a nice substitute.

Caprese Chicken and Orzo

PREP TIME: 20 Minutes • **START TO FINISH:** 40 Minutes • 4 servings

4 (about 5 oz each) boneless skinless chicken breasts

1 teaspoon salt

½ teaspoon pepper

2 tablespoons olive oil

1 cup chicken broth (from 14.5-oz can)

1 can (14.5 oz) fire-roasted diced tomatoes, undrained

1 cup uncooked orzo or rosa marina pasta (6 oz)

1 package (8 oz) mozzarella pearls or bocconcini (small fresh mozzarella cheese balls), drained

¼ cup shredded thinly sliced fresh basil leaves

1 Sprinkle both sides of chicken with ½ teaspoon of the salt and the pepper.

2 In 12-inch nonstick skillet, heat oil over medium-high heat. Add chicken; cook 3 to 4 minutes on each side or until browned. Remove chicken from skillet, place on heatproof plate.

3 Add broth, tomatoes, and remaining ½ teaspoon salt to skillet; heat to boiling. Stir in orzo; return to boiling. Place chicken on orzo. Reduce heat; cover.

4 Simmer 12 to 16 minutes or until most of liquid is absorbed, orzo is tender, and juice of chicken is clear when center of thickest part is cut (at least 165°F).

5 Top mixture with mozzarella pearls; cover. Cook over medium-low heat 2 to 4 minutes or until mozzarella slightly melts. Sprinkle with basil. Serve immediately.

1 Serving Calories 560; Total Fat 23g (Saturated Fat 2.5g, Trans Fat 0g); Cholesterol 140mg; Sodium 1,210mg; Total Carbohydrate 34g (Dietary Fiber 2g); Protein 53g **Carbohydrate Choices:** 2

Cooking without Nut Ingredients? Always read labels to make sure each ingredient is made without nuts. Products, ingredients, and processing methods can change.

flavor-packed
deliciousness

Don't let the ingredient list fool ya! This delish soup is literally thrown together in minutes. Top with sour cream, if ya like, and serve a crunchy salad alongside it. Dinner is done!

Chicken Tortilla Soup

PREP TIME: 10 Minutes ● **START TO FINISH:** 3 Hours 10 Minutes ●
8 servings (1¼ cups each)

1 lb boneless skinless chicken breasts

¾ teaspoon salt

½ teaspoon pepper

2 cups water

1½ cups chicken broth (from 32-oz carton)

1 can (14.5 oz) fire-roasted diced tomatoes, undrained

1 can (11 oz) whole kernel corn with red and green peppers, drained

1 can (10 oz) enchilada sauce

1 medium onion, chopped (1 cup)

1 can (4.5 oz) chopped green chiles

1 teaspoon ground cumin

1 teaspoon chili powder

4 cups tortilla chips, coarsely crushed

½ cup chopped fresh cilantro leaves

1 Spray 5- to 6-quart slow cooker with cooking spray. Place chicken in slow cooker, sprinkle with salt and pepper. Add remaining ingredients except tortilla chips and cilantro; cover.

2 Cook on Low heat setting 3 to 4 hours or until juice of chicken is clear when center of thickest part is cut (at least 165°F).

3 Remove chicken from slow cooker; place on cutting board. Cool slightly. Shred chicken using 2 forks. Return chicken to slow cooker. Gently stir in tortilla chips. Sprinkle with cilantro.

1 Serving Calories 210 (Calories from Fat 50); Total Fat 6g (Saturated Fat 1g, Trans Fat 0g); Cholesterol 35mg; Sodium 810mg; Total Carbohydrate 22g (Dietary Fiber 3g, Sugars 4g); Protein 15g **Carbohydrate Choices:** 1½

Cooking without Nut Ingredients? Always read labels to make sure each ingredient is made without nuts. Products, ingredients, and processing methods can change.

This flavorful meat loaf is sure to be a hit with mashed cauliflower or potatoes. Or, serve it cold the next day in a sandwich.

Turkey-Veggie Meat Loaf

PREP TIME: 20 Minutes • **START TO FINISH:** 1 Hour 25 Minutes •
6 servings

1 lb ground turkey (at least 93% lean)

1 cup shredded carrot (1 medium)

1 cup shredded zucchini (1 small)

¾ cup pure quick-cooking oats

¼ cup finely chopped onion

¾ teaspoon salt

½ teaspoon pepper

1 clove garlic, finely chopped

1 egg

⅓ cup strawberry fruit spread

2 tablespoons chili sauce

Chopped fresh parsley, if desired

1 Heat oven to 350°F. Spray 8×4-inch loaf pan with cooking spray without flour.

2 In large bowl, gently mix turkey, carrots, zucchini, oats, onion, salt, pepper, garlic, and egg. Spread mixture in pan. In small microwavable bowl, mix fruit spread and chili sauce; cover with plastic wrap. Microwave on High 30 to 60 seconds or until just bubbly; stir. Spread sauce evenly over top of meat loaf.

3 Bake uncovered 50 to 60 minutes or until instant-read meat thermometer inserted in center reads 165°F. Let stand 5 minutes.

4 Using knife, loosen meat loaf around edges of pan; remove from pan to cutting board. Sprinkle with chopped parsley; cut into slices.

1 Serving Calories 230; Total Fat 8g (Saturated Fat 2g, Trans Fat 0g); Cholesterol 90mg; Sodium 440mg; Total Carbohydrate 20g (Dietary Fiber 2g); Protein 18g **Carbohydrate Choices:** 1

Cooking without Dairy Ingredients? Always read labels to make sure each ingredient is made without dairy ingredients. Products, ingredients, and processing methods can change.

Cooking Gluten Free? Always read labels to make sure each recipe ingredient is gluten free. Products and ingredient sources can change.

Layer on the yum by adding ¼ cup grated Parmesan cheese and additional thinly sliced basil leaves, if you like.

Beef 🅐🅝🅓 Veggie Lasagna

PREP TIME: 25 Minutes • **START TO FINISH:** 1 Hour 15 Minutes •
8 servings

1 lb ground beef (at least 85% lean)

1 medium bell pepper (any color), chopped (1 cup)

1 medium onion, chopped (1 cup)

½ teaspoon salt

4 cups tomato and basil pasta sauce (from two 25.5-oz jars)

1 container (15 oz) whole milk ricotta cheese

2 eggs, slightly beaten

2 cups shredded mozzarella cheese (8 oz)

¼ cup chopped fresh basil leaves

6 oz uncooked oven-ready gluten-free brown rice lasagna noodles (about 8)

1 Heat oven to 375°F. Spray 13×9-inch (3-quart) glass baking dish with cooking spray.

2 In 12-inch skillet, cook beef, bell pepper, onion, and salt over medium-high heat 8 to 11 minutes, stirring occasionally, or until beef is thoroughly cooked; drain. Return beef mixture to skillet; stir in pasta sauce. Heat to boiling over medium-high heat; remove from heat.

3 Meanwhile, in medium bowl, stir together ricotta and eggs. Stir in 1 cup of the mozzarella cheese and the basil. Set aside.

4 Spread 2 cups beef mixture in baking dish; top with half of the noodles and 1¼ cups of the ricotta mixture. Spread 2 cups beef mixture over ricotta; top with remaining noodles. Top with remaining ricotta mixture and remaining beef mixture. Sprinkle with remaining 1 cup mozzarella cheese.

recipe continues

5   Cover; bake 40 minutes. Uncover; bake 10 minutes longer or until lasagna is hot and bubbly. Let stand 10 minutes before serving.

1 Serving Calories 460; Total Fat 24g (Saturated Fat 10g, Trans Fat 0.5g); Cholesterol 125mg; Sodium 750mg; Total Carbohydrate 35g (Dietary Fiber 3g); Protein 27g **Carbohydrate Choices:** 2

Cooking without Nut Ingredients? Always read labels to make sure each ingredient is made without nuts. Products, ingredients, and processing methods can change.
Cooking Gluten Free? Always read labels to make sure each recipe ingredient is gluten free. Products and ingredient sources can change.

What Is Soil?

Soil isn't just dirt that holds the roots of plants in place. Soil is a living ecosystem made up of little pieces of rock, sand, clay, pockets of air, water, and then billions of living organisms making their home in it. When that ecosystem is healthy and thriving, billions of living creatures—from bacteria to earthworms—can be found in a single teaspoon of soil. These creatures feed each other and keep one another healthy.

What Happens if Soil Isn't Healthy?

When healthy soil is full of living creatures, some of them provide important nutrients to plants through their roots, helping the plants grow and thrive. In turn, the plants make food for these creatures through their roots. It's another example of how biodiversity helps everyone. If soil isn't healthy, farmers have to feed the crops directly to keep them growing. That's not sustainable, either for the farmers (buying plant food is expensive!) or for the planet (making plant food uses lots of energy, and it pollutes the environment). Organic farmers believe that healthy soil means healthy plants means healthy people.

Go for the joy! Use meaty traditional ribs rather than the thinner Korean-style ribs for this finger-licking dish.

Slow-Cooker Barbecue Beef Short Ribs

PREP TIME: 20 Minutes • **START TO FINISH:** 8 Hours 20 Minutes •
6 servings

4 to 4½ lb bone-in beef short ribs, cut into individual ribs

½ teaspoon salt

½ teaspoon pepper

½ cup gluten-free beef broth (from 32-oz carton)

¾ cup sweet-and-spicy gluten-free barbecue sauce

2 tablespoons whole grain mustard

Sliced green onions, if desired

Mashed potatoes, if desired

1 Spray 5- to 6-quart slow cooker with cooking spray. Heat 12-inch nonstick skillet over medium-high heat. Season ribs with salt and pepper. Cook ribs in two batches, on all sides 2 to 3 minutes per side, until browned. Transfer ribs to slow cooker; discard fat and drippings.

2 In small bowl, mix broth, ½ cup of the barbecue sauce, and the mustard. Pour over ribs in slow cooker; cover. Cook on Low heat setting 8 to 9 hours or until tender.

3 With slotted spoon or tongs, carefully remove ribs to serving platter. In small microwavable bowl, heat remaining ¼ cup barbecue sauce covered on High 30 to 60 seconds or until heated through. Brush ribs with heated barbecue sauce; garnish with sliced onions. Serve with mashed potatoes.

1 Serving Calories 270; Total Fat 16g (Saturated Fat 6g, Trans Fat 0.5g); Cholesterol 80mg; Sodium 730mg; Total Carbohydrate 11g (Dietary Fiber 1g); Protein 21g **Carbohydrate Choices:** 1

Cooking without Nut Ingredients? Always read labels to make sure each ingredient is made without nuts. Products, ingredients, and processing methods can change.
Cooking Gluten Free? Always read labels to make sure each recipe ingredient is gluten free. Products and ingredient sources can change.

These homemade pizza rolls are easy to make, delicious to eat, and so versatile ya can serve them for lunch, dinner, or as a snack!

Air Fryer Pepperoni Pizza Crescent Rolls

PREP TIME: 10 Minutes ● **START TO FINISH:** 40 Minutes ● 8 servings
(1 crescent roll and 2 tablespoons sauce each)

1 can (8 oz) refrigerated Annie's organic crescent rolls (8 count)

24 slices pepperoni

½ cup shredded mozzarella cheese (2 oz)

1 cup tomato pasta or pizza sauce, heated

1 Cut 8-inch round of cooking parchment paper* and place in bottom of air fryer basket.

2 Unroll dough; separate into 8 triangles. Place 3 slices pepperoni, slightly overlapping, on center of each triangle. Top each with about 1 tablespoon cheese.

3 Roll up, starting at shortest side of triangle and rolling to opposite point. Place 4 crescent rolls point side down on parchment paper in air fryer basket. Place remaining crescent rolls on plate; cover with plastic wrap. Refrigerate while cooking first batch of rolls.

4 Set air fryer to 300°F. Cook 6 minutes. With tongs, turn rolls over. Cook 4 to 7 minutes longer or until golden brown. Remove from air fryer to serving plate; cover loosely with foil to keep warm. Unwrap remaining rolls. Place in air fryer as directed. Cook as directed.

5 Serve warm crescents with warm pasta sauce for dipping.

*For safety, do not heat the air fryer with just the parchment in basket. If you like, a 10-inch piece of foil can be used in place of the parchment paper. Spray it with cooking spray before adding crescent rolls to air fryer.

Easy Cooking Tip Air fryer temperature control settings vary according to brand and model. If your air fryer does not have the exact temperature setting called for in the recipe, consult your manual for suggested temperature settings.

1 Serving Calories 170; Total Fat 9g (Saturated Fat 4g, Trans Fat 0g); Cholesterol 10mg; Sodium 530mg; Total Carbohydrate 16g (Dietary Fiber 0g); Protein 4g **Carbohydrate Choices:** 1

Cleanup is simple if ya line the pan with regular or nonstick foil before baking.

Crunchy Panko Fish Nuggets
with Lemon-Dill Sauce

PREP TIME: 15 Minutes ● **START TO FINISH:** 35 Minutes ● 4 servings

Lemon-Dill Sauce
¼ cup mayonnaise

2 tablespoons plain yogurt

1 teaspoon chopped fresh or ¼ teaspoon dried dill weed

1 teaspoon lemon zest

2 teaspoons fresh lemon juice

Cooking without Nut Ingredients?
Always read labels to make sure each ingredient is made without nuts. Products, ingredients, and processing methods can change.

Fish Nuggets
3 tablespoons all-purpose flour

1 teaspoon garlic salt

1 teaspoon paprika

1 egg

2 tablespoons water

½ teaspoon red pepper sauce

1¼ cups plain panko crispy bread crumbs

3 tablespoons butter, melted

1 lb cod fillets (½ inch thick), cut into 1½-inch pieces

1 Heat oven to 425°F. Spray 15×10×1-inch pan with cooking spray. In small bowl, mix all sauce ingredients until blended. Cover and refrigerate until serving time.

2 In shallow bowl or pie plate, mix flour, garlic salt, and paprika. In another shallow bowl or pie plate, beat egg, water, and pepper sauce with whisk. In third shallow bowl or pie plate, mix bread crumbs and butter.

3 Coat fish with seasoned flour; dip into egg mixture. Coat with crumb mixture, pressing crumbs into fish; shake off excess. Place fish in pan.

4 Bake 15 to 20 minutes or until fish flakes easily with fork. Serve immediately with sauce.

1 Serving Calories 430; Total Fat 23g (Saturated Fat 8g, Trans Fat 0g); Cholesterol 125mg; Sodium 570mg; Total Carbohydrate 31g (Dietary Fiber 0g); Protein 27g **Carbohydrate Choices:** 2

Hack Your Mac

If ya love mac & cheese but want to take it on a flavor ride, we've got you covered. Having one or several of these add-ins available means each person in the family can customize their own bowl. It's so easy and so yum.

Make the mac & cheese as directed on the package, stir in any of the ingredients below, and dig in—or use it as a pizza or burger topping or as a taco filling.

VERY VEGGIE	MEAT IT UP
Chopped fresh or sun-dried (drained if in oil) tomato	Pepperoni
Chopped avocado	Cooked and crumbled sausage
Cooked sweet peas	Cooked and crumbled bacon
Chopped cooked broccoli	Cooked shredded barbecue chicken, beef, or pork
Chopped cooked asparagus	Buffalo chicken
Sliced green onions	Hot dogs
Chopped bell peppers (cooked or fresh)	Chicken nuggets
Cooked, mashed butternut or acorn squash or pumpkin	Drained, flaked tuna
Chopped fresh spinach, kale, or arugula leaves	Hot, cooked sloppy joes
Roasted Brussels sprouts	Chopped, cooked ham
Chopped marinated artichoke hearts	Cut-up cooked lobster or crab
Canned (drained) or fresh, cooked whole kernel sweet corn	

SEASONINGS AND SAUCES	OTHER TOPPINGS
Chopped fresh or dried basil leaves	Sliced or chopped pickles
Buffalo sauce	Green chiles or sliced fresh or pickled jalapeño
Salsa or pico de gallo	Shredded cheese, any flavor
Sriracha	Crushed croutons
Chopped fresh chives	¼ cup plain or Italian-style panko crispy bread crumbs cooked with 1 tablespoon melted butter over medium heat until toasted
Pesto	Crushed potato or tortilla chips

see photo on next page

mac with broccoli,
red bell pepper,
and buttery panko
topping
↓

burgers with mac & barbecue sauce

pepperoni & mac pizza

**comforting
cheesiness**

With the cheesy, homey goodness of this mac soup, you'll get requests to make this often. Sprinkle bowlfuls with some Annie's organic Cheddar Bunnies for a bit of crunchy bunny fun.

Easy Mac & Cheese Soup

PREP TIME: 20 Minutes • **START TO FINISH:** 25 Minutes • 4 servings (about 1¾ cups each)

2 tablespoons butter

1 medium onion, chopped (1 cup)

1 carton (32 oz) reduced-sodium chicken broth

1 cup milk

1 box (6 oz) Annie's Shells & Real Aged Cheddar macaroni & cheese

1 package (10 oz) broccoli florets, halved if large (about 3½ cups)

1 cup shredded carrot (1 medium)

1 cup shredded cheddar cheese (4 oz)

1 In 5-quart Dutch oven, heat butter over medium heat until melted. Add onion; cook, stirring frequently, 3 to 5 minutes or until softened.

2 Stir in broth, milk, pasta from box, broccoli, and carrots. Heat to boiling uncovered over high heat; reduce heat. Simmer 6 to 8 minutes, stirring frequently, or until pasta and broccoli are tender. Stir in powdered cheese packet from box and cheddar cheese until cheese is melted. Remove from heat. Serve immediately.

1 Serving Calories 430; Total Fat 20g (Saturated Fat 11g, Trans Fat 0.5g); Cholesterol 55mg; Sodium 1,110mg; Total Carbohydrate 43g (Dietary Fiber 4g); Protein 19g **Carbohydrate Choices:** 3

Boost the goodness in this dinner favorite by topping it with chopped fresh tomato. So good!

Bacon Avocado Mac & Cheese

PREP TIME: 10 Minutes • **START TO FINISH:** 25 Minutes • 2 servings

1 box (6 oz) Annie's Shells & Real Aged Cheddar macaroni & cheese

3 tablespoons milk

2 tablespoons butter

4 slices bacon, crisply cooked and crumbled

1 medium avocado, pitted, peeled, and cubed

1 tablespoon chopped fresh cilantro leaves

1 In 3-quart saucepan, prepare macaroni and cheese as directed on box using milk and butter.

2 Stir in bacon. Cook 2 to 3 minutes, stirring occasionally, until heated through. Gently stir in avocado. Sprinkle with cilantro.

1 Serving Calories 640; Total Fat 34g (Saturated Fat 14g, Trans Fat 0.5g); Cholesterol 60mg; Sodium 920mg; Total Carbohydrate 65g (Dietary Fiber 7g); Protein 20g **Carbohydrate Choices:** 4

Why Is Healthy Soil Important?

Healthy soil means seeds and seedlings have a better chance at being healthy and growing successfully. Animals that eat healthy plants are healthier. Successful organic farmers work hard to understand the ecosystem on their farm, from the unique needs of all creatures and plants that live and grow there to the soil and the water and how it flows over it.

Mac lovers will go nuts for this new way to enjoy mac & cheese in a veggie-loaded knife-and-fork sandwich.

Mac **&** Cheese Cali Sandwiches

PREP TIME: 15 Minutes • **START TO FINISH:** 25 Minutes • 4 sandwiches

1 box (6 oz) Annie's Shells & Real Aged Cheddar macaroni & cheese

3 tablespoons milk

2 tablespoons mayonnaise

2 tablespoons whole grain or Dijon mustard

8 slices whole grain bread, lightly toasted

4 leaves romaine lettuce, torn in half

1 medium plum (Roma) tomato, cut into 8 thin slices

½ cup shredded carrot

1 In 3-quart saucepan, heat 6 cups water to boiling. Add pasta from box. Cook 8 to 10 minutes, stirring occasionally, or until tender; drain. Return to pan; stir in milk and powdered cheese packet from box until well mixed.

2 In small bowl, mix mayonnaise and mustard. Spread 1 tablespoon mayonnaise mixture on each of 4 toasted bread slices. Top each with 2 romaine halves; spoon macaroni and cheese evenly over sandwiches. Top with tomatoes and carrots. Top each with a remaining slice of toasted bread; press each sandwich slightly. Cut sandwiches in half.

1 Sandwich Calories 420; Total Fat 11g (Saturated Fat 3g, Trans Fat 0g); Cholesterol 10mg; Sodium 860mg; Total Carbohydrate 64g (Dietary Fiber 7g); Protein 16g **Carbohydrate Choices:** 4

This is a dive-into meatless dish, or ya can pair it with your favorite chicken or meat for a more belly-filling feast.

Mac & Cheese with Peppers and Peas

PREP TIME: 15 Minutes • **START TO FINISH:** 30 Minutes • 2 servings

1 box (6 oz) Annie's organic Shells & Real Aged Cheddar macaroni & cheese

½ cup milk

2 tablespoons butter

¼ cup chopped red bell pepper

½ cup frozen sweet peas, thawed

1 cup finely shredded sharp cheddar cheese (4 oz)

½ cup Annie's organic Cheddar Bunnies, crushed (from 7.5-oz box)

1 In 3-quart saucepan, prepare macaroni and cheese as directed on box, using milk and butter. Remove from heat.

2 Stir in bell pepper, peas, and ¾ cup of the cheese until well mixed. Cook over medium-low heat 3 to 4 minutes, stirring occasionally, or until heated through and cheese is melted.

3 In small bowl, mix remaining ¼ cup cheese and the crackers until well mixed. Sprinkle evenly over shells mixture.

1 Serving Calories 790; Total Fat 40g (Saturated Fat 22g, Trans Fat 1g); Cholesterol 105mg; Sodium 1230mg; Total Carbohydrate 78g (Dietary Fiber 6g); Protein 29g **Carbohydrate Choices:** 5

Fresh and flavorful noodles make for a comforting, homemade meal in minutes. For a little crunch, top with coarsely chopped gluten-free cocktail or dry-roasted peanuts.

Thai-Style Noodles and Veggies

PREP TIME: 30 Minutes • **START TO FINISH:** 30 Minutes • 4 servings (1¼ cups each)

1 package (8 oz) pad Thai rice noodles

½ cup creamy organic peanut butter

½ cup water

3 tablespoons fresh lime juice

2 tablespoons gluten-free soy sauce

¼ teaspoon crushed red pepper flakes

1 tablespoon canola oil

4 medium green onions, sliced (¼ cup)

2 cups spiralized or shredded zucchini (about 2 medium)

2 cups matchstick carrots (from 10-oz bag)

1 In 5-quart Dutch oven, cook noodles as directed on package; drain.

2 In large microwavable bowl, mix peanut butter, water, lime juice, soy sauce, and pepper flakes. Microwave uncovered on High 30 to 60 seconds or just until hot. Stir with whisk until well blended. Add noodles to sauce; gently toss until evenly coated. Cover and keep warm.

3 In same Dutch oven, heat oil over medium-high heat. Reserve 1 tablespoon of green onions. Add zucchini, carrots, and remaining green onions. Cook uncovered, stirring frequently, 3 to 5 minutes or until vegetables are crisp-tender. Remove from heat.

4 Stir noodle mixture into vegetable mixture in Dutch oven until well mixed. Sprinkle with reserved green onions. Serve immediately.

1 Serving Calories 510; Total Fat 21g (Saturated Fat 3.5g, Trans Fat 0g); Cholesterol 0mg; Sodium 950mg; Total Carbohydrate 66g (Dietary Fiber 6g); Protein 13g **Carbohydrate Choices:** 4½

Cooking without Dairy Ingredients? Always read labels to make sure each ingredient is made without dairy ingredients. Products and ingredients can change.

Cooking Gluten Free? Always read labels to make sure each recipe ingredient is gluten free. Products and ingredient sources can change.

Cooking Vegetarian or Vegan? Always read labels to make sure each recipe ingredient is vegetarian or vegan. Products and ingredient sources can change.

How Do Farmers Keep Soil Healthy?

There are lots of ways that farmers keep soil healthy, and they're all important. Organic farmers don't use chemicals that only feed the plants and can harm the creatures in the soil. They feed the creatures in the soil with natural fertilizers like manure and compost, which also help the plants grow. Sometimes organic farmers grow crops just for the purpose of feeding the soil organisms and adding nutrients to the soil—these are called cover crops.

Picky eaters have met their match! Hummus, made from chickpeas, adds extra goodness to the barbecue sauce, and they won't even know it's there.

Veggie Nuggets ⬤with Barbecue-Hummus Dipping Sauce

PREP TIME: 25 Minutes ● **START TO FINISH:** 1 Hour 30 Minutes ●
4 servings (5 nuggets and 2 tablespoons sauce each)

Veggie Nuggets
⅔ cup yellow split peas, sorted, rinsed

3 cups fresh cauliflower florets, cooked

½ teaspoon salt

¼ teaspoon garlic-pepper blend

¼ cup plain or Italian-style bread crumbs

2 tablespoons water

½ cup cooked fresh or frozen sweet peas

Hummus Dipping Sauce
¼ cup hummus (from 10-oz container)

¼ cup Carolina or regular barbecue sauce

1 In 2-quart saucepan, place split peas; add cold water to cover. Heat to boiling. Reduce heat; cover. Simmer 35 to 40 minutes or until split peas are soft but not mushy. Drain.

2 Heat oven to 425°F. Line 15×10×1-inch pan with cooking parchment paper or heavy-duty foil; spray with cooking spray.

3 In food processor, place split peas, cauliflower, salt, and garlic pepper. Cover; process with 10 to 15 on-and-off pulses or until finely chopped. Add bread crumbs and water. Cover; process with a few pulses until mixture just holds together. Stir in peas.

recipe continues

4 For each nugget, shape about 2 tablespoons pea mixture into 2×1-inch oval. Place 1 inch apart on pan. Spray nuggets with cooking spray.

5 Bake 17 to 22 minutes, turning once, or until light golden brown.

6 In small bowl, mix hummus and barbecue sauce until blended. Serve with warm nuggets.

1 Serving Calories 220; Total Fat 2.5g (Saturated Fat 0g, Trans Fat 0g); Cholesterol 0mg; Sodium 640mg; Total Carbohydrate 39g (Dietary Fiber 12g); Protein 11g **Carbohydrate Choices:** 2½

Cooking without Dairy or Nut Ingredients? Always read labels to make sure each ingredient is made without dairy or nuts. Products, ingredients, and processing methods can change.
Cooking Vegetarian? Always read labels to make sure each recipe ingredient is vegetarian. Products and ingredient sources can change.

What Is an Ecosystem?

Organisms are living things. They can be so small we can't see them or as large as an elephant! Plants and animals are also organisms. Did you know no single organism can exist on its own? All living things need millions of other organisms to survive. An ecosystem is a community of interacting organisms and their environment.

Sweets to Bring Smiles

Xanthan gum is made from fermented corn sugar and is safe to eat. It's commonly used when baking gluten free to replicate the texture you'd get in traditionally baked goods made with gluten. You can leave it out of this recipe, if you wish, but the cookies will be more delicate, somewhat like a shortbread cookie.

Fruit-Filled Oatmeal Thumbprint Cookies

PREP TIME: 30 Minutes • **START TO FINISH:** 2 Hours • 32 cookies

Cookies
¾ cup vegan buttery sticks, softened
½ cup packed brown sugar
1½ teaspoons vanilla
1 egg yolk
1½ cups pure oat flour

½ cup pure rolled oats
¾ teaspoon xanthan gum
½ teaspoon salt
¼ teaspoon ground cinnamon

Filling
½ cup fruit spread (any flavor)

1 In large bowl, beat buttery sticks, sugar, and vanilla with electric mixer on medium speed until fluffy. Beat in egg yolk until smooth. Beat in oat flour, oats, xanthan gum, salt, and cinnamon until soft dough forms. Cover and refrigerate at least 1 hour or until firm.

2 Heat oven to 375°F.

3 Shape dough into 1-inch balls. Onto each of 2 ungreased cookie sheets, place 12 balls about 2 inches apart. Press thumb into center of each cookie to make indentation, but do not press all the way to the cookie sheet.

4 Bake 1 cookie sheet 9 to 11 minutes or until edges begin to brown. Immediately gently remake indents with end of wooden spoon handle. Let stand 2 minutes; remove cookies from cookie sheet to cooling rack. Repeat with second cookie sheet.

recipe continues

5 Meanwhile, onto completely cooled cookie sheet, repeat with remaining dough as directed in step 3. Bake cookies as directed in step 4. Cool completely, about 15 minutes. Fill each thumbprint with about ½ teaspoon fruit spread. Store loosely covered in single layer at room temperature up to 2 days.

Easy Cooking Tip Organic sugar granule size can differ among manufacturers. Be sure to use a fine crystal granulated sugar for the cookies for the best texture; coarse crystal sugars do not dissolve as easily during baking. For a little sparkle, roll the dough balls in a shallow bowl or pie plate containing 2 to 3 teaspoons of organic sugar before placing on cookie sheets.

1 Cookie Calories 90; Total Fat 4.5g (Saturated Fat 1.5g, Trans Fat 0g); Cholesterol 5mg; Sodium 85mg; Total Carbohydrate 11g (Dietary Fiber 0g); Protein 1g **Carbohydrate Choices:** 1

Cooking without Dairy or Nut Ingredients? Always read labels to make sure each ingredient is made without dairy or nuts. Products, ingredients, and processing methods can change.

Cooking Gluten Free? Always read labels to make sure each recipe ingredient is gluten free. Products and ingredient sources can change.

Cooking Vegetarian? Always read labels to make sure each recipe ingredient is vegetarian. If unsure about an ingredient or product, check with the manufacturer.

Insects as Organic Farmers' Little Helpers

Some insects don't eat nectar from flowers; instead, they eat smaller bugs. And some of the smaller bugs like to eat the crops that the farmer grows. Ladybugs and wasps are some of the insects that help farmers by eating bugs, like aphids, that feed on their crops. It's another example of why protecting biodiversity on the farm is so important for organic farmers.

How Plants Grow

Plants need air, water, and food to grow well, just like you. Using the energy from the sunlight on their leaves, plants take carbon dioxide from the air and combine it with water to make sugars that are full of energy. These sugars are some of the basic building blocks for the plant's own body (it's what they use to grow more and bigger roots, stems or trunks, and leaves). But plants need other nutrients as well. If a plant only had sunlight, water, and air, it wouldn't grow. Just like you, plants also need food!

Everybunny's going to be caught with their hand in the cookie jar with these yummy and wholesome treats.

Vegan Chocolate Chip Cookies

PREP TIME: 45 Minutes • **START TO FINISH:** 1 Hour • 40 cookies

⅔ cup refined coconut oil, melted

⅔ cup vegan granulated sugar

⅔ cup packed vegan brown sugar

½ cup unsweetened vanilla almond milk

2 teaspoons vanilla

2½ cups all-purpose flour

1 teaspoon baking soda

1 teaspoon baking powder

½ teaspoon salt

1 bag (10 oz) vegan semisweet chocolate chips

1 Heat oven to 350°F.

2 In large bowl, stir coconut oil, granulated sugar, and brown sugar until well mixed. Stir in almond milk and vanilla. Stir in flour, baking soda, baking powder, and salt until dough forms. Stir in chocolate chips.

3 Onto each of 2 ungreased cookie sheets, drop dough by slightly rounded tablespoonfuls 2 inches apart.

4 Bake 1 cookie sheet 11 to 14 minutes or until edges are light brown and tops look set. Let stand 1 minute; remove from cookie sheet to cooling rack. Repeat with second cookie sheet.

5 Meanwhile, onto completely cooled cookie sheets, repeat with remaining dough as directed in step 3. Bake cookies as directed in step 4. Cool completely. Store in tightly covered container.

1 Cookie Calories 130; Total Fat 6g (Saturated Fat 4.5g, Trans Fat 0g); Cholesterol 0mg; Sodium 95mg; Total Carbohydrate 17g (Dietary Fiber 0g); Protein 1g **Carbohydrate Choices:** 1

Cooking without Dairy or Nut Ingredients? Always read labels to make sure each ingredient is made without dairy or nuts. Products, ingredients, and processing methods can change.

Cooking Vegetarian or Vegan? Always read labels to make sure each recipe ingredient is vegetarian or vegan. If unsure about an ingredient or product, check with the manufacturer.

photo on next page

Powerful Pollinators

Pollination is another example of why biodiversity is so important for agriculture—imagine if farmers had to add "go from flower to flower to pollinate" on their daily to-do list. There are more than 100 crops that wouldn't grow well without pollinators, so protecting insects is a key part of biodiversity on farms.

melt-in-your-mouth
yumminess

Vegan Chocolate Chip Cookies

Part crispies, part Scotcheroos, this fun twist adds the goodness of Cinna Bunnies cereal, fruit snacks, and dried strawberries into a new bar nobunny can resist! Be sure to use a large bowl for melting the marshmallows since they may "grow" in the microwave as they soften.

Bunny Scotcheroo-Crispies

PREP TIME: 15 Minutes ● **START TO FINISH:** 1 Hour 15 Minutes ● 32 bars

1 package (10 oz) miniature marshmallows

¼ cup butter

4½ cups Annie's organic Cinna Bunnies cinnamon cereal

½ cup freeze-dried strawberries (from 1.2-oz package)

4 pouches Annie's organic Summer Strawberry fruit snacks (from 4-oz box)

1½ cups semisweet chocolate chips

½ cup creamy peanut butter

1 Spray 13×9-inch (3-quart) pan with cooking spray or line with foil; spray with cooking spray.

2 In large microwavable bowl, place marshmallows and butter. Microwave uncovered on High 1 minute; stir. Microwave an additional 30 seconds to 1 minute or until most of the marshmallows are melted.

3 Add cereal, strawberries, and fruit snacks; stir until evenly coated. Spray back of spoon with cooking spray. Using back of spoon, press mixture firmly into pan.

4 In small microwavable bowl, place chocolate chips and peanut butter. Microwave uncovered on High 1 minute; stir well. Microwave about 1 minute longer, stirring every 30 seconds or until mixture can be stirred smooth.

5 Spread evenly over cereal mixture. Refrigerate about 1 hour or until chocolate mixture is set. Cut into 8 rows by 4 rows. Store in an airtight container in refrigerator up to 5 days.

1 Bar Calories 140; Total Fat 6g (Saturated Fat 2.5g, Trans Fat 0g); Cholesterol 0mg; Sodium 65mg; Total Carbohydrate 20g (Dietary Fiber 1g); Protein 1g **Carbohydrate Choices:** 1

Once the foil is in the pan, spray it with cooking spray. This will make the bars release easily from the foil.

Apricot-Chocolate Snack Bars

PREP TIME: 15 Minutes ● **START TO FINISH:** 45 Minutes ● 18 bars

2 cups Annie's organic Cocoa Bunnies cereal

½ cup chopped dried apricots or mangoes (from 6-oz package)

½ cup lightly salted cashew pieces

⅓ cup honey

2 tablespoons butter

1 teaspoon vanilla

1 Line 9×5-inch loaf pan with 15×12-inch piece of foil. Spray foil with cooking spray.

2 In medium bowl, stir cereal, apricots, and cashew pieces until mixed. Set aside.

3 In 1-quart saucepan, heat honey and butter over medium heat about 3 minutes, stirring occasionally, or until mixture is boiling and foamy. Boil 2 minutes, stirring frequently. Remove from heat; stir in vanilla. Stir honey mixture into cereal mixture until evenly coated.

4 Press into pan. Fold edges of foil over cereal; press evenly and firmly. Unwrap foil from top of bars. Refrigerate about 30 minutes or until firm. Remove from pan; fold back foil. Cut crosswise into 1-inch slices; cut each slice lengthwise in half. Store in an airtight container in refrigerator up to 5 days.

1 Bar Calories 80; Total Fat 3.5g (Saturated Fat 1g, Trans Fat 0g); Cholesterol 0mg; Sodium 55mg; Total Carbohydrate 12g (Dietary Fiber 0g); Protein 1g **Carbohydrate Choices:** 1

What Is Composting?

Composting is like recycling, but for things that come from living creatures, like plants and animals. Farmers can compost the parts of the crops they don't use and the manure from the animals they raise. When these things decompose, or break down over time, they turn into rich, dark soil known as compost. When farmers add compost to their fields, it's one of the many ways they keep the ground healthy—it feeds the living creatures in the soil.

You can compost at home too! When you collect leaves or grass clippings from your yard and food scraps like banana peels, apple cores, and egg shells in a special bin, they turn into compost. Composting your food scraps not only supports soil health, but it also means you're keeping waste out of landfills.

These whole-grain, blondie-like bars get their rich texture from brown sugar. Using light brown sugar will ensure the bars don't get too dark.

Snickerdoodle Jam Bars

PREP TIME: 20 Minutes • **START TO FINISH:** 1 Hour 50 Minutes • 16 bars

⅔ cup packed brown sugar

⅓ cup vegan buttery sticks, softened

1 egg

1 teaspoon vanilla

1½ cups white whole wheat flour

1 teaspoon cream of tartar

¾ teaspoon baking soda

½ teaspoon salt

⅔ cup raspberry fruit spread

2 teaspoons granulated sugar

¼ teaspoon ground cinnamon

1 Heat oven to 350°F. Spray 8-inch baking pan with cooking spray or grease with buttery sticks.

2 In large bowl, mix brown sugar and buttery sticks with spoon until blended. Add egg and vanilla; mix until slightly fluffy.

3 Stir in flour, cream of tartar, baking soda, and salt until crumbly and well mixed. Press 1½ cups of the dough into pan. Spoon fruit spread evenly over dough in pan. Crumble remaining dough over fruit mixture. In small bowl, stir granulated sugar and cinnamon until blended. Sprinkle sugar mixture over dough.

4 Bake 26 to 30 minutes or until top is dry and set when touched lightly. Cool completely, about 1 hour. Using knife, loosen edges from pan. Cut into 4 rows by 4 rows. Store loosely covered at room temperature up to 3 days.

1 Bar Calories 150; Total Fat 4.5g (Saturated Fat 1.5g, Trans Fat 0g); Cholesterol 10mg; Sodium 180mg; Total Carbohydrate 25g (Dietary Fiber 1g); Protein 2g **Carbohydrate Choices:** 1½

Cooking without Dairy or Nut Ingredients? Always read labels to make sure each ingredient is made without dairy or nuts. Products, ingredients, and processing methods can change.
Cooking Vegetarian? Always read labels to make sure each recipe ingredient is vegetarian. Products and ingredient sources can change.

Organic brown sugar brands will vary in crystal size, with some being coarser than others. If you use a coarse-textured sugar, the toffee will be somewhat sandy-textured—but still totally yummy!

Fruit-Graham Toffee Bars

PREP TIME: 20 Minutes ● **START TO FINISH:** 3 Hours 5 Minutes ● 16 bars

6 honey graham cracker rectangles (from 14.4-oz box)

½ cup butter

½ cup packed brown sugar

4 oz plain cream cheese spread (from 8-oz container)

½ cup nonfat Greek vanilla yogurt

1 pack Annie's organic fruit Strawberry Splits Peel-A-Parts (from 3.3-oz box)

2 pouches Annie's organic Bees, Bugs & Butterflies fruit snacks (from 4-oz box)

¼ cup fresh or freeze-dried raspberries

¼ cup fresh or freeze-dried blueberries

1 Heat oven to 350°F. Line 9-inch square pan with heavy duty foil, leaving 2-inch overhang on two opposite sides of pan for easy removal. Place graham crackers in single layer, cutting a few as needed to cover bottom of pan (reserve any unused pieces for another use); set aside.

2 In 2-quart saucepan, heat butter and brown sugar over medium heat about 3 minutes until mixture boils and begins to foam. Boil 2 minutes longer, stirring constantly. Pour evenly over graham crackers; spread to cover. Bake 9 to 10 minutes or until bubbly. Cool in pan completely, about 45 minutes.

3 In small bowl, mix cream cheese and yogurt until smooth. Spread over toffee. Cover and refrigerate at least 2 hours but no longer than 24 hours. Just before serving, separate peel-aparts into strings; arrange randomly on yogurt mixture. Arrange fruit snacks and fruit on yogurt mixture. Cut into 4 rows by 4 rows.

1 Bar Calories 150; Total Fat 9g (Saturated Fat 5g, Trans Fat 0g); Cholesterol 25mg; Sodium 105mg; Total Carbohydrate 16g (Dietary Fiber 0g); Protein 1g **Carbohydrate Choices:** 1

Power of Plants

Plants are pretty amazing because they can make sugars or carbohydrates from sunlight and water and use carbon dioxide in the air. But plants need other nutrients for their leaves, stems, and roots to grow. They get these nutrients from the soil, using their roots to soak them up. But did you know that plants and the tiny creatures living in the soil work together to help one another out? Plants send some of the sugars they produce through their roots to feed the tiny creatures living in the soil, which in return help the plant out by giving them nutrients that the plant can't make on its own.

Don't be surprised if you have to use more natural plant-based food coloring to color coconut or frosting than traditional food color. For a deeper, truer color, we call for natural orange food color powder for the carrots. Look for it in some discount stores, natural food stores, or online.

Bunny ⬤ Carrot Brownies

PREP TIME: 50 Minutes • **START TO FINISH:** 1 Hour 45 Minutes •
20 carrot cookies and 8 bunny cookies

Brownies

1 box (18.3 oz) Annie's organic Double Chocolate brownie mix

½ cup butter, melted

1 tablespoon water

1 egg

Frosting and Decorations

2 cups powdered sugar

½ cup butter, softened

2 tablespoons milk

1 teaspoon vanilla

1¼ teaspoons natural orange food color powder

6 tablespoons plus 2 teaspoons unsweetened shredded coconut

¼ teaspoon green plant-based food coloring

20 miniature marshmallows

16 candy eye decorations

1 teaspoon pink decorating sugar

1 Heat oven to 350°F. Line 13×9-inch baking pan with foil, leaving 2-inch overhang on two opposite sides of pan for easy removal. Spray bottom and sides of foil with cooking spray.

2 In medium bowl, mix all brownie ingredients until blended. Spread in pan.

3 Bake 18 to 22 minutes or until set when lightly touched. Cool completely, about 30 minutes. For easy cutting, freeze uncovered in pan 20 minutes.

recipe continues

4 Meanwhile, in medium bowl, beat powdered sugar, butter, milk, and vanilla with electric mixer on low speed until blended. Beat on medium speed about 1 minute or until smooth. Set aside.

5 Lift foil from pan, place on cutting board. Fold back foil; cut brownies into 3 long rectangles, using a sharp knife. Peel foil from brownies.

6 For carrots, cut 2 of the brownie rectangles into 10 triangles with each triangle having a 2-inch base. Reserve scraps for another use. In small bowl, stir ¾ cup of the frosting and orange food color powder until blended. Place orange frosting in quart-size resealable food-storage plastic bag. With scissors, cut one tiny corner off bag. Squeeze bag to pipe frosting over top of each brownie triangle. In small bowl, stir 2 tablespoons of the coconut and green food coloring until evenly mixed. Place on wide end of carrots for carrot greens.

7 For bunnies, cut remaining brownie rectangle crosswise into 8 rectangles. In small bowl, place 2 teaspoons of the frosting; set aside. Frost brownies with remaining frosting; sprinkle with 4 tablespoons of the coconut.

8 Frost 8 of the marshmallows with reserved 2 teaspoons of frosting; roll in remaining 2 teaspoons coconut. Place a marshmallow on top of each brownie, near a short end, for tail. For the pink noses, cut 4 marshmallows in half horizontally. Dip cut end of each marshmallow in pink decorating sugar. Place one on top of each brownie, sugar side up, near a short end. Press 2 candy eye decors behind the noses for eyes. For ears, cut remaining 8 marshmallows horizontally in half. Press one side of each marshmallow into pink decorating sugar. Press 2 marshmallow halves, sugar side up, behind eyes. Store any remaining brownies loosely covered in single layer in container for up to 2 days.

1 Brownie Calories 190; Total Fat 9g (Saturated Fat 6g, Trans Fat 0g); Cholesterol 25mg; Sodium 100mg; Total Carbohydrate 24g (Dietary Fiber 0g); Protein 1g **Carbohydrate Choices:** 1½

We've got ya covered. Arrange the cookies on top of the brownie batter so that each brownie will end up with a cookie when they are cut. That way, nobunny will feel left out.

Granola and Chocolate Chip–Topped Brownies

PREP TIME: 10 Minutes ● **START TO FINISH:** 2 Hours 15 Minutes ●
16 brownies

1 box (18.3 oz) Annie's organic Double Chocolate brownie mix

½ cup butter, melted

1 tablespoon water

2 eggs

2 Annie's organic Chocolate Chip chewy granola bars, crumbled (from 5.34-oz box)

16 Annie's organic Chocolate Chip Cookie Bites (from 6.5-oz box)

1 Heat oven to 350°F. Spray bottom of 9-inch baking pan with cooking spray.

2 In medium bowl, stir together brownie mix, butter, water, and eggs. Spread evenly in pan. Sprinkle top of batter with granola bars; arrange cookie bites evenly over top.

3 Bake 32 to 35 minutes or until toothpick inserted 2 inches from the center of the pan comes out almost clean.

4 Cool completely on cooling rack, about 1 hour 30 minutes. Cut into 4 rows by 4 rows.

1 Brownie Calories 260; Total Fat 13g (Saturated Fat 7g, Trans Fat 0g); Cholesterol 40mg; Sodium 170mg; Total Carbohydrate 33g (Dietary Fiber 1g); Protein 2g **Carbohydrate Choices:** 2

Plant a Bee-Friendly Garden

You can help out pollinators where you live by planting a bee-friendly garden. Bee-friendly gardens have lots of flowering plants that provide food for pollinators, as well as fresh water and places for wild bees to live. If you have a lawn, ask your parents to leave flowers like dandelions and clover. You can also plant some native plants that are good food for pollinators. And of course, just like organic farmers, only use organic and natural methods to deal with unwanted weeds and insects.

Are you curious to know which plants are pollinator-friendly? The Xerces Society, a nonprofit organization that protects wildlife, is a great resource!

Oooh my! These decadent brownies also have the added goodness of zucchini. We've cut these amazing brownies into pieces even little bunnies can hold. The little leftover niblets are small enough to satisfy a sweet tooth but not ruin dinner. Or ya can skip the cutting and just grab a fork and dive in.

Earth Day Zucchini Brownies

PREP TIME: 30 Minutes ● **START TO FINISH:** 3 Hours 10 Minutes ●
20 brownies

Brownies
1 box (18.3 oz) Annie's organic Double Chocolate brownie mix

½ cup butter, melted

1 tablespoon water

2 eggs

1 cup coarsely shredded zucchini (about 1 small)

½ cup miniature semisweet chocolate chips

Frosting
2 cups powdered sugar

½ cup butter, softened

2 tablespoons milk

1 teaspoon vanilla

½ to ¾ teaspoon green plant-based food coloring

½ to ¾ teaspoon blue plant-based food coloring

1 Heat oven to 350°F. Line bottom of 9-inch round cake pan with cooking parchment paper; spray with cooking spray.

2 In medium bowl, mix brownie mix, butter, water, and eggs; stir until well blended. Stir in zucchini and chocolate chips. Spread in pan.

3 Bake 35 to 38 minutes or until toothpick inserted 3 inches from side of pan comes out almost clean. Cool until warm, about 1 hour 30 minutes; invert onto serving plate. Remove parchment. Cool completely, about 30 minutes.

4 In medium bowl, beat powdered sugar, butter, milk, and vanilla with electric mixer on low speed until blended. Beat on medium speed about 1 minute or until smooth. In small bowl, spoon half of the frosting. Stir green food coloring into 1 bowl of frosting until

recipe continues

well mixed and blue food coloring to other bowl of frosting until well mixed.

5 Frost top of brownie with green frosting to look like the land portions of a globe. Frost remaining top of brownie and sides with blue frosting to resemble the water portions of a globe. Cut into 4 rows by 5 rows. Refrigerate in covered container up to 3 days.

1 Brownie Calories 280; Total Fat 14g (Saturated Fat 8g, Trans Fat 0g); Cholesterol 45mg; Sodium 150mg; Total Carbohydrate 35g (Dietary Fiber 1g); Protein 1g **Carbohydrate Choices:** 2

Pretty Flowers

Brightly colored flowers aren't just pretty to us; bees and other insects love them too. They know the bright colors of the flowers mean they'll find nectar in them to drink. And when they do so, they carry pollen from the flowers to other plants. When a plant has been pollinated, that flower can grow into fruit or seeds.

Lots of yummy foods, like apples, berries, and pumpkins, start out as flowers on plants. Those flowers can turn into fruits and vegetables only if they receive pollen from other plants nearby. Nature does this easily, when insects move between plants and carry pollen from one flower to another. In turn, the plants reward the insects for doing this important job for them by feeding them nectar from the flowers.

hidden veggie goodness

HAPPY EARTH DAY

Fun between Dinner and Dessert

When dinner is finished but you're not ready to enjoy dessert yet, keep the conversation and connection going with any of these creative ways to have fun either inside or outside the house. No one will want to turn to TV or their phones to pass time when the local entertainment is so captivating!

Flower Power

Set up the frosted (but not decorated) Fruity Cupcakes (page 175) with bowls of berries or cut-up fresh fruit and let everyone decorate their own cupcakes. Get creative by making flowers, bugs, or any design with the fruit.

Outdoor Scavenger Hunt

Teach kiddos about the environment and appreciating green spaces and nature by going to a neighborhood park to play a trash/recycling scavenger hunt game. Talk about the importance of trees, pointing out flowers and dandelions you see along the way.

Where Does Food Come From?

Test your knowledge about where different foods come from or what foods various animals produce. Have your kiddo get their hands dirty by planting a vegetable in a glass jar to learn what happens under the soil as well as above it.

Pack Lunches

Involve everybunny in packing up lunches for the next day. It's a great way to use leftovers as well as get creative with snacks. As kids get involved in selecting and preparing food, their curiosity buds and they try new foods. Check out the yummy recipes in the Shareable Snacks (page 52) chapter as well as this one.

Build a Fort

Use the living room or space under the kitchen table to build a fun fort with blankets and pillows. It's a great place to read a book!

Couch Karaoke

Let your couch be your stage and a spoon be your microphone! Turn on the tunes and sing along. Ya might want to video this. . . . It's bound to be a memory in the making.

Outdoor Scavenge
✽ ✽ ✽ ✽ ✽

☐ Pop Can
☐ Plasite Bags   ☐ New.
☐ Food Cartou   ☐ Card

These irresistible cuties have the bonus of hidden butternut squash—and you'd never know it. Use up leftover cooked squash for these cupcakes or cook fresh or frozen squash. Mash and cool it before using and it stealthily becomes part of the cupcakes.

Fruity Cupcakes

PREP TIME: 20 Minutes ● **START TO FINISH:** 1 Hour 20 Minutes ●
24 cupcakes

Cupcakes

1 box (21 oz) Annie's organic Classic yellow cake mix

1 cup milk

¾ cup mashed cooked and cooled butternut squash

¾ cup canola oil

1 tablespoon lemon zest

1 tablespoon fresh lemon juice

4 eggs

Frosting and Fruit

1 package (8 oz) cream cheese, softened

½ cup powdered sugar

1 tablespoon milk

1 tablespoon fresh lemon juice

1½ to 2 cups fresh berries or assorted cut-up fruit

1 Heat oven to 350°F. Place paper baking cup in each of 24 regular-size muffin cups.

2 In large bowl, beat all cupcake ingredients with electric mixer on low speed 30 seconds. Beat on high speed 2 minutes, scraping bowl occasionally. Divide batter evenly among baking cups, filling each about three-fourths full.

3 Bake 15 to 20 minutes or until toothpick inserted in center comes out clean. Cool 10 minutes; remove from pan. Cool completely, about 30 minutes.

4 In small bowl, beat cream cheese, powdered sugar, milk, and lemon juice with an electric mixer on medium speed about 1 minute or until light and creamy. Frost cupcakes. Top with berries.

1 Cupcake Calories 220; Total Fat 11g (Saturated Fat 3g, Trans Fat 0g); Cholesterol 40mg; Sodium 170mg; Total Carbohydrate 27g (Dietary Fiber 0g); Protein 3g **Carbohydrate Choices:** 2

Whether the perfect Valentine goodie or a way for kids to learn the alphabet, these heart-shaped treats are a cinch to make without needing a special pan.

Sweetheart Cupcakes

PREP TIME: 55 Minutes • **START TO FINISH:** 1 Hour 45 Minutes •
24 cupcakes

Cupcakes
1 box (21 oz) Annie's organic Classic yellow cake mix

1 cup water

¾ cup canola oil

4 eggs

Strawberry Filling
1 package (10 oz) frozen sliced strawberries, thawed

1 tablespoon honey

Frosting
2 oz white chocolate baking bar, chopped (from 4-oz package)

3 tablespoons heavy whipping cream

⅓ cup butter, softened

2 cups powdered sugar

1 Heat oven to 350°F. Place paper baking cup in each of 24 regular-size muffin cups. Cut two 12×12-inch pieces of foil. Cut each piece into six 2-inch strips; cut each strip in half. Roll each piece of foil into a ball, about ¾ inch in diameter; set aside.

2 In large bowl, beat cupcake ingredients with electric mixer on low speed 30 seconds, scraping bowl occasionally. Beat on high speed 2 minutes. Divide batter evenly among muffin cups. Place a foil ball between each paper baking cup and muffin cup to form heart shape.

3 Bake 18 to 22 minutes or until toothpick inserted in center comes out clean. Cool 10 minutes; remove from pan to cooling rack. Cool completely, about 45 minutes.

4 Meanwhile, in food processor or blender, place strawberries. Cover; process strawberries about 30 seconds or until smooth. Pour into

recipe continues

sweet
surprise

2-quart saucepan; stir in honey. Heat uncovered over medium-low heat, stirring occasionally, until boiling. Continue cooking, stirring frequently, 15 minutes or until mixture is thickened. Remove from heat. Spoon into small heatproof bowl. Refrigerate uncovered until chilled, about 45 minutes, stirring twice to speed cooling.

5 In small microwavable bowl, microwave white chocolate and 2 tablespoons of the whipping cream uncovered on High 30 seconds; stir until smooth. Cool 5 minutes. In medium bowl, beat butter and 1 cup of the powdered sugar with electric mixer on medium speed until blended. Add white chocolate mixture and remaining 1 tablespoon whipping cream; mix well. Add remaining 1 cup powdered sugar; beat until smooth.

6 To make holes in cupcakes, slowly spin end of round handle of wooden spoon back and forth in the center, making an indentation almost to the bottom of each cupcake. Spoon about 2 tablespoons filling into 1-pint resealable food-storage plastic bag; set aside. Spoon remaining filling into another 1-pint resealable food-storage plastic bag. Cut about ¼ inch off corner of bag. Gently push cut corner of bag into center of cupcake. Squeeze fruit mixture into center of each cupcake to fill holes.

7 Frost each cupcake with about 1 tablespoon frosting. Snip small corner from remaining bag of fruit mixture. Onto each cupcake, gently squeeze bag to write a letter, symbol, or word. Store loosely covered at room temperature up to 3 days.

1 Cupcake Calories 250; Total Fat 12g (Saturated Fat 3g, Trans Fat 0g); Cholesterol 40mg; Sodium 160mg; Total Carbohydrate 35g (Dietary Fiber 0g); Protein 2g **Carbohydrate Choices:** 2

Protecting Pollinators

Farmers rely on pollinators to help their crops grow, so it's important for them to take steps to protect them. Farmers can plant pollinator-friendly plants on their land that are good sources of pollen and nectar. Trees are also good for pollinators. Pollinators get nectar from trees' flowers, leaves, and resin. Trees provide nesting materials, and holes in the trees are great shelters for pollinators. Organic farmers only use organic products and natural solutions to improve the soil to help keep pollinators healthy.

Keep these cuties on hand for a perfect creamy, dreamy summertime snack or dessert. If ya like a brighter berry color, mix ½ teaspoon beet juice with the yogurt before spooning into the cups.

Frozen Yogurt Mini Pies

PREP TIME: 15 Minutes ● **START TO FINISH:** 1 Hour 20 Minutes ●
15 mini pies

6 honey graham cracker rectangles, finely crushed (about ¾ cup; from 14.4-oz box)

2 tablespoons butter, melted

2 containers (6 oz each) original mixed-berry yogurt

15 fresh blueberries or raspberries

1 Place mini paper baking cup in each of 15 mini muffin cups.

2 In small bowl, stir graham cracker crumbs and butter until well mixed. Spoon and press 1 tablespoon mixture into bottom of each muffin cup. Top each with 1 rounded tablespoon yogurt and 1 berry.

3 Freeze about 1 hour or until frozen. Let stand 5 minutes at room temperature before serving.

Easy Cooking Tip If you like, keep the frozen pies stashed in a freezer-safe food storage container in the freezer up to 1 month by loosely covering the pies with plastic wrap before covering with lid. Pull out as many as you would like at a time and let them soften slightly as directed in step 3 before serving.

1 Mini Pie Calories 50; Total Fat 2g (Saturated Fat 1g, Trans Fat 0g); Cholesterol 5mg; Sodium 45mg; Total Carbohydrate 7g (Dietary Fiber 0g); Protein 1g **Carbohydrate Choices:** ½

Cooking Vegetarian? Always read labels to make sure each recipe ingredient is vegetarian. Products and ingredient sources can change.

Mango and kiwifruit pair up with granola bars for a refreshing, fruity treat with a fun crunch. Peaches or nectarines can be substituted for the mango. Feel free to use what is in season or on sale.

Creamy Fruit (and) Granola Pops

PREP TIME: 15 Minutes • **START TO FINISH:** 4 Hours 20 Minutes •
6 pops

1¼ cups whole milk vanilla yogurt

¾ cup frozen mango chunks, chopped (from 10- to 12-oz bag)

1 tablespoon honey

1 kiwifruit, peeled, chopped (½ cup)

2 Annie's organic Chocolate Chip chewy granola bars, crumbled (from 5.34-oz box)

6 wooden craft sticks or plastic spoons

1 In blender, place yogurt, ¼ cup of the mango, and the honey. Cover; blend on high speed about 1 minute or until smooth. Stir in remaining ½ cup mango and kiwifruit.

2 Divide mixture evenly among 6 (5-oz) paper cups. Sprinkle crumbled granola bars over tops of pops. Insert craft stick or spoon in center of each pop. Freeze uncovered about 4 hours or until frozen.

3 Let stand 5 minutes at room temperature before serving. Tear off paper cups.

1 Pop Calories 120; Total Fat 3g (Saturated Fat 1.5g, Trans Fat 0g); Cholesterol 5mg; Sodium 50mg; Total Carbohydrate 20g (Dietary Fiber 1g); Protein 2g **Carbohydrate Choices:** 1

These versatile parfaits are a sweet surprise in a lunch box (pack in an insulated container) or when you're having friends or family over. Pint size or full size, all bunnies will love them.

Raspberry–Banana Split Parfaits

PREP TIME: 15 Minutes ● **START TO FINISH:** 15 Minutes ● 6 parfaits

Whipped Cream
1 cup heavy whipping cream
2 tablespoons powdered sugar
1 teaspoon vanilla

Parfaits
2 cups vanilla pudding
1 cup fresh raspberries
1 ripe medium banana, thinly sliced
¾ cup Annie's organic Chocolate Bunny Grahams (from 7.5-oz box)
Additional Annie's organic Chocolate Bunny Grahams and fresh raspberries, if desired

1 In chilled medium bowl, beat whipping cream, powdered sugar, and vanilla with electric mixer on high speed. Beat until stiff peaks form.

2 In each of 6 (6-oz) glasses, layer ⅓ cup pudding and ⅓ cup whipped cream. Top with raspberries, banana slices, and bunny grahams. Divide remaining whipped cream among glasses. Garnish with additional bunny grahams and raspberries. Serve immediately or refrigerate up to 4 hours.

1 Parfait Calories 300; Total Fat 15g (Saturated Fat 9g, Trans Fat 0.5g); Cholesterol 50mg; Sodium 300mg; Total Carbohydrate 35g (Dietary Fiber 2g); Protein 4g **Carbohydrate Choices:** 2

Bring even more smiles by topping the bananas with a dollop of sweetened whipped cream, ice cream, or vanilla yogurt and a sprinkle of additional spice. Dreamy!

Honey-Chai Panfried Bananas

PREP TIME: 10 Minutes • **START TO FINISH:** 10 Minutes • 2 servings

2 tablespoons butter
2 tablespoons honey
½ teaspoon ground ginger
¼ teaspoon ground cardamom
¼ teaspoon ground cinnamon

⅛ teaspoon pepper
Dash ground cloves
2 ripe, firm medium bananas, cut in half lengthwise

1 In 10-inch nonstick skillet, melt butter over medium heat. Stir in all ingredients except bananas.

2 Place bananas in skillet. Cook 2 to 3 minutes, carefully turning bananas once halfway through cooking with nonstick pancake turner, until bananas are softened and heated through. Remove from heat.

3 Divide bananas and syrup between 2 dessert plates. Serve warm.

Easy Cooking Tip When purchasing bananas, look for ones that are just ripe so that they are still firm. The firmness makes slicing and turning them in the pan easy, so they don't break apart.

1 Serving Calories 290; Total Fat 12g (Saturated Fat 7g, Trans Fat 0g); Cholesterol 30mg; Sodium 95mg; Total Carbohydrate 45g (Dietary Fiber 3g); Protein 1g **Carbohydrate Choices:** 3

Cooking without Nut Ingredients? Always read labels to make sure each recipe ingredient is made without nuts. Products, ingredient sources, and processing methods can change.

Cooking Gluten Free? Always read labels to make sure each recipe ingredient is gluten free. Products and ingredient sources can change.

Cooking Vegetarian? Always read labels to make sure each recipe ingredient is vegetarian. If unsure about an ingredient or product, check with the manufacturer.

Microwaving the honey mixture until it comes to a full boil will ensure most of the pumpkin seeds will cling to the other ingredients and not fall to the bottom of the bowl.

Bunny Blitz Mix

PREP TIME: 15 Minutes • **START TO FINISH:** 30 Minutes • 20 servings (½ cup each)

5 cups Annie's organic Birthday Cake cereal

2 cups Annie's organic Chocolate Bunny Grahams (from 7.5-oz box)

¾ cup roasted salted hulled pumpkin seeds (pepitas)

¼ cup butter

¼ cup honey

1 cup vanilla- or chocolate-flavored bite-size cookie wafers (from 8.82-oz bag)

1 cup miniature marshmallows

1 box (4 oz) Annie's organic Berry Patch fruit snacks (5 pouches)

1 In large microwavable bowl, mix cereal, bunny grahams, and pumpkin seeds.

2 In 2-cup microwavable measuring cup, microwave butter and honey on High 1 to 2 minutes, stirring every 30 seconds, until mixture comes to a full boil and butter is melted. Pour over cereal mixture. Stir until cereal mixture is evenly coated. Microwave on High 2 minutes, stirring after 1 minute.

3 Spread slightly (leaving some clumps) on waxed paper or foil. Cool about 15 minutes. Break any large pieces slightly; place in serving bowl. Toss with cookie wafers, marshmallows, and fruit snacks. Store in airtight container up to 3 days.

1 Serving Calories 170; Total Fat 6g (Saturated Fat 2g, Trans Fat 0g); Cholesterol 5mg; Sodium 90mg; Total Carbohydrate 26g (Dietary Fiber 1g); Protein 2g **Carbohydrate Choices:** 2

(GF)
(V)
(V+)

What apples make the best apple crisp? Granny Smith, Braeburn, or Honeycrisp apples would work well in this tummy-tickling treat.

Skillet Apple Crisp

PREP TIME: 30 Minutes • **START TO FINISH:** 1 Hour • 12 servings

Topping

½ cup gluten-free all-purpose rice flour blend

2 tablespoons packed organic brown sugar

1 teaspoon ground cinnamon

¼ teaspoon salt

¼ cup unsalted coconut oil, very cold, cut into small pieces

¾ cup pure old-fashioned oats

½ cup pecans, chopped

Filling

5 to 6 tart baking apples (Granny Smith or Rome), peeled and sliced thinly (about 8 cups)

⅓ cup packed organic brown sugar

2 tablespoons gluten-free all-purpose rice flour blend

1 teaspoon ground cinnamon

¼ teaspoon salt

1 Heat oven to 375°F.

2 In food processor, place rice flour blend, brown sugar, cinnamon, and salt. Cover; pulse several times to blend. Add coconut oil pieces; pulse until distinct crumbs form. In large bowl, place flour blend mixture; stir in oats and pecans. Set aside.

3 Spray 12-inch cast-iron skillet or 13×9-inch (3-quart) baking dish with cooking spray. In large bowl, mix filling ingredients; toss to blend. Arrange filling evenly in skillet. Sprinkle topping evenly over apples, pressing lightly.

4 Bake 40 to 45 minutes or until topping is golden brown and apples are tender (cover with foil if top begins to brown too fast). Serve warm.

1 Serving Calories 190; Total Fat 8g (Saturated Fat 4.5g, Trans Fat 0g); Cholesterol 0mg; Sodium 130mg; Total Carbohydrate 27g (Dietary Fiber 2g); Protein 1g **Carbohydrate Choices:** 2

Cooking without Dairy Ingredients? Always read labels to make sure each ingredient is made without dairy ingredients. Products, ingredients, and processing methods can change.

Cooking Gluten Free? Always read labels to make sure each recipe ingredient is gluten free. Products and ingredient sources can change.

Cooking Vegetarian or Vegan? Always read labels to make sure each recipe ingredient is vegetarian or vegan. Products and ingredient sources can change.

photo on next page

Visit a Farm

Do you want to see some of the crops and animals that come from farms up close? Put on your overalls and take an educational farm tour! You might get to milk a cow, ride a pony, or harvest apples, peas, or berries. See chickens—can you walk like a chicken? You might get to see or feed goats—what do they like to eat? Talk about what you hear, see, taste, smell, touch. Check online for farms you can visit near you.

Skillet Apple Crisp

Shop Local

One of the best ways to connect with the farms growing your food is to buy directly from local farmers. This helps the community where you live, as it creates jobs for farmers. Help your parents pick out healthy food from farmers' markets. Some farms offer CSA shares—that stands for community-supported agriculture—where you'll get a box full of delicious fresh foods every week. You might just find some new foods to love!

Bibliography

"Banana." Britannica Kids, accessed April 20, 2022, https://kids.britannica.com/kids/article/banana/352822.

"A Bee Is More than a Bug." Climate Kids, accessed April 18, 2022, https://climatekids.nasa.gov/bees/#:~:text=Loss%20of%20the%20bees'%20habitat,able%20to%20fend%20off%20diseases.

"California Agricultural Production Statistics." California Department of Food and Agriculture, accessed April 20, 2022, https://www.cdfa.ca.gov/Statistics/.

Capehart, Tom, and Susan Proper. "Corn Is America's Largest Crop in 2019" (Research and Science blog post). US Department of Agriculture, accessed April 20, 2022, https://www.usda.gov/media/blog/2019/07/29/corn-americas-largest-crop-2019#:~:text=Update%3A%20In%20July%2C%20USDA's%20National,and%20soybeans%20in%2014%20states.

"Farm to Table: A Play on Farm to School at Home." Action for Healthy Kids, accessed April 20, 2022, https://www.actionforhealthykids.org/activity/farm-to-table-a-play-on-farm-to-school-at-home/.

"How Plants Grow: Lessons for Kids." Study.com, accessed April 18, 2022, https://study.com/academy/lesson/how-plants-grow-lesson-for-kids.html.

"Organic Farms Facts for Kids." Kiddle, accessed April 18, 2022, https://kids.kiddle.co/Organic_farms.

"Plants and Growth." TheSchoolRun.com, accessed April 18, 2022, https://www.theschoolrun.com/homework-help/plants-and-growth.

"Pollinators." US Department of Agriculture, accessed April 18, 2022, https://www.usda.gov/pollinators.

"The Story of Wheat for Kids." Nebraska Wheat, accessed April 20, 2022, https://nebraskawheat.com/wp-content/uploads/2014/01/StoryOfWheat.pdf.

"10 Ways to Save the Bees." Bee Conservancy, accessed April 18, 2022, https://thebeeconservancy.org/10-ways-to-save-the-bees/.

Index

Note: Page references in *italics* indicate photographs.

A

Agriculture, 6, 106
Almond butter
    Apple Nachos, *58,* 59
    Nutty Almond Butter Pancakes,
        10–11, *12–13*
Apples
    Apple-and-Sausage-Stuffed French Toast,
        28–29, *29*
    Apple Nachos, *58,* 59
    Skillet Apple Crisp, 190–91, *192*
Apricot-Chocolate Snack Bars, 154, *155*
Avocado Bacon Mac & Cheese, 130, *131*

B

Bacon
    Bacon Avocado Mac & Cheese, 130, *131*
    Easy Breakfast Sandwiches, *38,* 39
Bananas
    about, 50
    Chocolate-Banana Bunny Shakes, 74, *75*
    Frozen Cocoa Bunny–Banana Pops, *54,* 55
    Honey-Chai Panfried Bananas, 186, *187*
    Lava Smoothies, 80–81, *81*
    Nutty Almond Butter Pancakes, 10–11,
        12–13
    Raspberry–Banana Split Parfaits, *184,* 185
    Ultimate Breakfast Smoothie Bowls, *42,* 43
Bars
    Apricot-Chocolate Snack Bars, 154, *155*
    Bunny and Carrot Brownies, 163–64, *165*
    Bunny Scotcheroo-Crispies, *152,* 153
    Earth Day Zucchini Brownies, 169–70, *171*
    Fruit-Graham Toffee Bars, 160, *161*
    Granola and Chocolate Chip–Topped
        Brownies, *166,* 167
    Snickerdoodle Jam Bars, *158,* 159

Beef
    Beef and Veggie Lasagna, *114,* 115–16
    Slow-Cooker Barbecue Beef Short Ribs,
        118, 119
Bee-friendly gardens, 168
Belgian Waffles, 16, *17*
Bento boxes, 70
Berries. See also specific berries
    Belgian Waffles, 16, *17*
    Churro French Toast Sticks with Berry
        Sauce, 25–27, *26*
    Cinnamon Roll Waffles, *18,* 19
    Fruity Cupcakes, *172–74,* 175
Biodiversity, 104, 117, 146, 149
Blueberries
    Blueberry Grape Smoothie Poppers,
        44–45, *46*
    Blueberry-Peach Smoothies, *76,* 77
    Frozen Yogurt Mini Pies, *180,* 181
    Fruit-Graham Toffee Bars, 160, *161*
    Nutty Almond Butter Pancakes,
        10–11, *12–13*
    Oatmeal Pancakes, *14,* 15
    Ultimate Breakfast Smoothie Bowls, *42,* 43
Bread. *See* French toast
Breakfast skills, 30–31
Broccoli
    Easy Mac & Cheese Soup, *128,* 129
    Parmesan Chicken Fingers and Roasted
        Veggies, 105–6, *107*
Brownies
    Earth Day Zucchini Brownies, 169–70, *171*
    Granola and Chocolate Chip–Topped
        Brownies, *166,* 167
Bunny Grahams
    Bunny Blitz Mix, *188,* 189
    Cobweb Crunch Mix, 68, *69*

Peanut Butter Graham Spinners, *62,* 63
Raspberry–Banana Split Parfaits, *184,* 185

C
Carrots
  Carrot Mango Smoothie Poppers, 44–45, *47*
  Easy Mac & Cheese Soup, *128,* 129
  Mac & Cheese Cali Sandwiches, *132,* 133
  Thai-Style Noodles and Veggies, 136–37, *137*
  Turkey-Veggie Meat Loaf, 112, *113*
Cereal
  Apple Nachos, *58,* 59
  Apricot-Chocolate Snack Bars, 154, *155*
  Bunny Blitz Mix, *188,* 189
  Bunny Scotcheroo-Crispies, *152,* 153
  Chocolate-Banana Bunny Shakes, 74, *75*
  Cinna Buddies–Muddy Buddy Mix, *66,* 67
  Frozen Cocoa Bunny-Banana Pops, *54,* 55
  Sweet and Salty Snack Mix, 64, *65*
  Watermelon Birthday Cake Shakes, *72,* 73
Cheddar Bunnies
  Cheddar Cracker Chicken Tenders,
    102, 103
  Mac & Cheese with Peppers and Peas,
    134, *135*
  Sweet and Salty Snack Mix, 64, *65*
Cheese. *See also* Cream cheese; Mac & cheese
  Air Fryer Pepperoni Pizza Crescent Rolls,
    120–21, *121*
  Beef and Veggie Lasagna, *114,* 115–16
  Buffalo Chicken Bites, *88,* 89
  Caprese Chicken and Orzo, 108–9, *109*
  Cheesy Piglets in a Blanket, 90, *91*
  Easy Baked Mozzarella Bites, 86, *87*
  Easy Breakfast Sandwiches, *38,* 39
  Grilled Mexican-Inspired Chicken
    Sandwiches, *98,* 99
  Herbed Goat Cheese Pizza Poppers, *92,* 93
  Mediterranean Watermelon Fries with
    Creamy Feta Dip, 60, *61*
  Monte Cristo Wafflewiches, *22,* 23
  Parmesan Chicken Fingers and Roasted
    Veggies, 105–6, *107*
Chicken
  Buffalo Chicken Bites, *88,* 89
  Caprese Chicken and Orzo, 108–9, *109*
  Cheddar Cracker Chicken Tenders, *102,* 103
  Chicken Tortilla Soup, *110,* 111
  Grilled Mexican-Inspired Chicken
    Sandwiches, *98,* 99

Parmesan Chicken Fingers and Roasted
  Veggies, 105–6, *107*
Three-Ingredient Sweet and Spicy Pulled
  Chicken, 96, *97*
Chicken sausages
  Apple-and-Sausage-Stuffed French Toast,
    28–29, *29*
  Easy Chicken Sausage Mac, 100, *101*
Chocolate. *See also* White chocolate
  Apricot-Chocolate Snack Bars, 154, *155*
  Bunny and Carrot Brownies, 163–64, *165*
  Bunny Scotcheroo-Crispies, *152,* 153
  Chocolate-Banana Bunny Shakes, 74, *75*
  Earth Day Zucchini Brownies, 169–70, *171*
  Granola and Chocolate Chip-Topped
    Brownies, *166,* 167
  Vegan Chocolate Chip Cookies, 148–
    49, *150–51*
Cinnamon
  Churro French Toast Sticks with Berry
    Sauce, 25–27, *26*
  Cinna Buddies–Muddy Buddy Mix, *66,* 67
Cinnamon rolls
  Cinnamon Roll Waffles, *18,* 19
  5-Ingredient Raspberry–Cream Cheese
    Cinnamon Roll Bake, 36, *37*
  Fruity Bunny Cinnamon Rolls, *34,* 35
Coconut
  Bunny and Carrot Brownies, 163–64, *165*
  Oatmeal Pancakes, *14,* 15
Composting, 156–57
Cookies
  Bunny Blitz Mix, *188,* 189
  Fruit-Filled Oatmeal Thumbprint Cookies,
    144, 145–46
  Granola and Chocolate Chip-Topped
    Brownies, *166,* 167
  Vegan Chocolate Chip Cookies, 148–
    49, *150–51*
Corn
  Chicken Tortilla Soup, *110,* 111
  organic corn, 24
Cover crops, 138
Crackers. *See* Cheddar Bunnies
Cream cheese
  Buffalo Chicken Bites, *88,* 89
  5-Ingredient Raspberry–Cream Cheese
    Cinnamon Roll Bake, 36, *37*
  Fruit-Graham Toffee Bars, 160, *161*
  Fruity Bunny Cinnamon Rolls, *34,* 35

Fruity Cupcakes, *172–74*, 175
   Granola Breakfast Pizzas, 40, *41*
Creative entertainment, 172
Crescent rolls
   Air Fryer Pepperoni Pizza Crescent Rolls,
      120–21, *121*
   Buffalo Chicken Bites, *88*, 89
   Cheesy Piglets in a Blanket, 90, *91*
   Easy Baked Mozzarella Bites, 86, *87*
Crop farmers, 84
Crops, 8, 20, 27, 104, 149
Cupcakes
   Fruity Cupcakes, *172–74*, 175
   Sweetheart Cupcakes, 176–78, *177*

D

Dairy farms, 77, 84

E

Ecosystem, 140
Eggs
   Easy Breakfast Sandwiches, *38*, 39
   Skillet Breakfast Mac & Cheese Bake,
      48, 49–50

F

Farmers and farming, 6, 27, 55, 64, 77, 78, 84,
      191, 194. *See also* Organic farms
Fish Nuggets, Crunchy Panko, with Lemon-
      Dill Sauce, *122*, 123
Flowers, 170
French toast
   Apple-and-Sausage-Stuffed French Toast,
      28–29, *29*
   Churro French Toast Sticks with Berry
      Sauce, 25–27, *26*
Fruit. See also specific fruits
   California fruit and nuts, 90
   Creamy Fruit and Granola Pops, 182,
      183
   Fruity Cupcakes, *172–74*, 175
   Granola Breakfast Pizzas, 40, *41*
Fruit snacks
   Bunny Blitz Mix, *188*, 189
   Bunny Scotcheroo-Crispies, *152*, 153
   Cinna Buddies–Muddy Buddy Mix, *66*, 67
   Cobweb Crunch Mix, 68, *69*
   Fruit-Graham Toffee Bars, 160, *161*
   Peanut Butter Graham Spinners, *62*, 63
   Sweet and Salty Snack Mix, 64, *65*

Fruit spread
   Fruit-Filled Oatmeal Thumbprint Cookies,
      144, 145–46
   Fruity Bunny Cinnamon Rolls, *34*, 35
   PB and J Waffle Toast, 20, *21*
   Snickerdoodle Jam Bars, *158*, 159

G

Gardens, 11, 100, 168
Graham crackers. *See also* Bunny Grahams
   Frozen Yogurt Mini Pies, *180*, 181
   Fruit-Graham Toffee Bars, 160, *161*
   Peanut Butter Graham Spinners, *62*, 63
   Strawberry-Lemon Frozen Yogurt
      Bark, 56, *57*
Granola bars
   Creamy Fruit and Granola Pops, 182, *183*
   Granola and Chocolate Chip–Topped
      Brownies, *166*, 167
   Granola Breakfast Pizzas, 40, *41*
   PB and J Waffle Toast, 20, *21*
   Ultimate Breakfast Smoothie Bowls, *42*, 43

H

Ham
   Monte Cristo Wafflewiches, *22*, 23
Hot dogs
   Cheesy Piglets in a Blanket, 90, *91*

M

Mac & cheese
   add-in ingredients for, 124–25
   Bacon Avocado Mac & Cheese, 130, *131*
   Easy Chicken Sausage Mac, 100, *101*
   Easy Mac & Cheese Soup, *128*, 129
   Mac & Cheese Cali Sandwiches, *132*, 133
   Mac & Cheese with Peppers and Peas,
      134, *135*
   Mac & Double Cheese Sticks, *82*, 83–84
   Skillet Breakfast Mac & Cheese Bake,
      48, 49–50
Mango
   Carrot Mango Smoothie Poppers, 44–45, *47*
   Creamy Fruit and Granola Pops, 182, *183*
   Mango Green Smoothies, 78, *79*
Marshmallows
   Bunny and Carrot Brownies, 163–64, *165*
   Bunny Blitz Mix, *188*, 189
   Bunny Scotcheroo-Crispies, *152*, 153
Meat Loaf, Turkey-Veggie, 112, *113*

N

Noodles and Veggies, Thai-Style, 136–37, *137*
Nuts
   grown in California, 90
   Nutty Almond Butter Pancakes,
      10–11, *12–13*
   Sweet and Salty Snack Mix, 64, *65*

O

Oats
   Fruit-Filled Oatmeal Thumbprint Cookies,
      144, 145–46
   Oatmeal Pancakes, *14,* 15
   Skillet Apple Crisp, 190–91, *192*
Orchards, 89
Organic farms, 85, 106, 117, 130, 138, 146
Organic foods, 24, 45, 85

P

Pancakes
   Fruity Alphabet Pancakes, 7–8, *9*
   Nutty Almond Butter Pancakes,
      10–11, *12–13*
   Oatmeal Pancakes, *14,* 15
Parfaits, Raspberry–Banana Split, *184,* 185
Pasta. *See also* Mac & cheese
   Beef and Veggie Lasagna, *114,* 115–16
   Caprese Chicken and Orzo, 108–9, *109*
Peaches
   Blueberry-Peach Smoothies, *76,* 77
   Fruity Alphabet Pancakes, 7–8, *9*
Peanut butter
   Bunny Scotcheroo-Crispies, *152,* 153
   PB and J Waffle Toast, 20, *21*
   Peanut Butter Graham Spinners, *62,* 63
   Thai-Style Noodles and Veggies, 136–37, *137*
   Ultimate Breakfast Smoothie Bowls, *42,* 43
Peas
   Mac & Cheese with Peppers and Peas,
      134, *135*
   Veggie Nuggets with Barbecue-Hummus
      Dipping Sauce, 139–40, *141*
Pepperoni Pizza Crescent Rolls, Air Fryer,
   120–21, *121*
Peppers
   Beef and Veggie Lasagna, *114,* 115–16
   Herbed Goat Cheese Pizza Poppers, *92,* 93
   Mac & Cheese with Peppers and Peas,
      134, *135*

Pies, Frozen Yogurt Mini, *180,* 181
Pizzas, Granola Breakfast, 40, *41*
Plants, 8, 11, 116, 117, 147, 162
Pollinators, 149, 168, 170, 179
Popcorn
   Cobweb Crunch Mix, 68, *69*
   Sweet and Salty Snack Mix, 64, *65*
Pops
   Creamy Fruit and Granola Pops, 182, *183*
   Frozen Cocoa Bunny-Banana Pops, *54,* 55
   Smoothie Poppers, 44–45, *46–47*
Pork. *See* Bacon; Ham; Pork sausages
Pork sausages
   Air Fryer Pepperoni Pizza Crescent Rolls,
      120–21, *121*
   Skillet Breakfast Mac & Cheese Bake,
      48, 49–50
Poultry farms, 64, 84
Pretzels
   Cinna Buddies–Muddy Buddy Mix, *66,* 67
   Cobweb Crunch Mix, 68, *69*
   Peanut Butter Graham Spinners, *62,* 63
   Sweet and Salty Snack Mix, 64, *65*

R

Ranches, 78, 84
Raspberries
   5-Ingredient Raspberry–Cream Cheese
      Cinnamon Roll Bake, 36, *37*
   Frozen Yogurt Mini Pies, *180,* 181
   Fruit-Graham Toffee Bars, 160, *161*
   Raspberry–Banana Split Parfaits, *184,* 185
   Ultimate Breakfast Smoothie Bowls, *42,* 43
Regenerative agriculture, 106

S

Sandwiches
   Easy Breakfast Sandwiches, *38,* 39
   Grilled Mexican-Inspired Chicken
      Sandwiches, *98,* 99
   Mac & Cheese Cali Sandwiches, *132,* 133
   Monte Cristo Wafflewiches, *22,* 23
Sausages. *See* Chicken sausages; Pork
   sausages
School gardens, 100
Shakes
   Chocolate-Banana Bunny Shakes, 74, *75*
   Watermelon Birthday Cake Shakes, *72,* 73
Smoothie Bowls, Ultimate Breakfast, *42,* 43
Smoothie Poppers, 44–45, *46–47*

Smoothies
    Blueberry-Peach Smoothies, *76,* 77
    Lava Smoothies, 80–81, *81*
    Mango Green Smoothies, 78, *79*
Snack mixes
    Bunny Blitz Mix, *188,* 189
    Cinna Buddies–Muddy Buddy Mix, *66,* 67
    Cobweb Crunch Mix, 68, *69*
    Sweet and Salty Snack Mix, 64, *65*
Soil, 116, 117, 130, 138, 156–57, 162
Soups
    Chicken Tortilla Soup, *110,* 111
    Easy Mac & Cheese Soup, *128,* 129
Spinach
    Easy Chicken Sausage Mac, 100, *101*
    Lime Green Smoothie Poppers, 44–45, *46*
    Mango Green Smoothies, 78, *79*
Squash. *See also* Zucchini
    Fruity Cupcakes, *172–74,* 175
Strawberries
    Apple Nachos, *58,* 59
    Bunny Scotcheroo-Crispies, *152,* 153
    Chocolate-Banana Bunny Shakes, 74, *75*
    Cinna Buddies–Muddy Buddy Mix, *66,* 67
    Fruity Alphabet Pancakes, 7–8, *9*
    Strawberry-Lemon Frozen Yogurt
        Bark, 56, *57*
    Sweetheart Cupcakes, 176–78, *177*

T

Tomatoes
    Caprese Chicken and Orzo, 108–9, *109*
    Chicken Tortilla Soup, *110,* 111
    Mac & Cheese Cali Sandwiches, *132,*
        133
Tortilla Chicken Soup, *110,* 111
Turkey
    Monte Cristo Wafflewiches, *22,* 23
    Turkey-Veggie Meat Loaf, 112, *113*

V

Vegetables. See also specific vegetables
    Parmesan Chicken Fingers and Roasted
        Veggies, 105–6, *107*
    Veggie Nuggets with Barbecue-Hummus
        Dipping Sauce, 139–40, *141*

W

Waffles
    Belgian Waffles, 16, *17*
    Cinnamon Roll Waffles, *18,* 19
    Monte Cristo Wafflewiches, *22,* 23
    PB and J Waffle Toast, 20, *21*
Watermelon
    Mediterranean Watermelon Fries with
        Creamy Feta Dip, 60, *61*
    Watermelon Birthday Cake Shakes, *72,* 73
Wheat and flour, 51
White chocolate
    Cinna Buddies–Muddy Buddy Mix, *66,* 67
    Sweetheart Cupcakes, 176–78, *177*

Y

Yogurt
    Belgian Waffles, 16, *17*
    Blueberry-Peach Smoothies, *76,* 77
    Creamy Fruit and Granola Pops, 182, *183*
    Frozen Cocoa Bunny–Banana Pops, *54,* 55
    Frozen Yogurt Mini Pies, *180,* 181
    Fruit-Graham Toffee Bars, 160, *161*
    Granola Breakfast Pizzas, 40, *41*
    Lava Smoothies, 80–81, *81*
    Mango Green Smoothies, 78, *79*
    Mediterranean Watermelon Fries with
        Creamy Feta Dip, 60, *61*
    Smoothie Poppers, 44–45, *46–47*
    Strawberry-Lemon Frozen Yogurt
        Bark, 56, *57*
    Ultimate Breakfast Smoothie Bowls, *42,* 43
    Watermelon Birthday Cake Shakes, *72,* 73

Z

Zucchini
    Earth Day Zucchini Brownies, 169–70, *171*
    Thai-Style Noodles and Veggies, 136–37, *137*
    Turkey-Veggie Meat Loaf, 112, *113*

Metric Conversion Guide

Weight

U.S. UNITS	CANADIAN METRIC	AUSTRALIAN METRIC	UK METRIC
1 ounce	30 g	30 g	25 g
2 ounces	55 g	60 g	55 g
3 ounces	85 g	90 g	85 g
4 ounces (¼ pound)	115 g	115 g	115 g
8 ounces (½ pound)	225 g	225 g	225 g
16 ounces (1 pound)	455 g	450 g	450 g

Volume

U.S. UNITS	CANADIAN METRIC	AUSTRALIAN METRIC	UK METRIC
⅛ teaspoon	1 mL	1 ml	1 ml
½ teaspoon	2 mL	2 ml	2.5 ml
1 teaspoon	5 mL	5 ml	5 ml
1 tablespoon	15 mL	20 ml	15 ml
¼ cup	50 mL	60 ml	60 ml
⅓ cup	75 mL	80 ml	80 ml
½ cup	125 mL	125 ml	125 ml
⅔ cup	150 mL	170 ml	150 ml
¾ cup	175 mL	190 ml	175 ml
1 cup	250 mL	250 ml	250 ml
1 quart	1 liter	1 liter	1 liter
1½ quarts	1.5 liter	1.5 liters	1.5 liters
½ gallon (2 quarts)	2 liters	2 liters	2 liters
2½ quarts	2.5 liters	2.5 liters	2.5 liters
3 quarts	3 liters	3 liters	3 liters
1 gallon (4 quarts)	4 liters	4 liters	4 liters

Note: The recipes in this cookbook have not been developed or tested using metric measures. When converting recipes to metric, some variations in quality may be noted.